An Expository Dictionary
of
Old Testament Words

BY W. E. Vine

An Expository Dictionary of New Testament Words
An Expository Dictionary of Old Testament Words
(edited by F. F. Bruce)

An Expository Dictionary
of
Old Testament Words

W. E. VINE, M.A.

Edited by F. F. BRUCE

FLEMING H. REVELL COMPANY
OLD TAPPAN, NEW JERSEY

An Expository Dictionary of Old Testament Words is
published in the United Kingdom by Marshall, Morgan
& Scott, Publications, Ltd.

Unless otherwise identified, Scripture quotations in this volume are from
the King James Version of the Bible (KJV).
Scripture quotations identified R.V. are from the Revised Version, 1881–
1885.
The Chart of Historical Comparisons is from *Let's Know the Bible* by John
W. Cawood, © 1971, published by Fleming H. Revell Company, and is used
by permission of the author.

Library of Congress Cataloging in Publication Data

Vine, William Edwy, 1873-1949.
   An expository dictionary of Old Testament words.

   Bibliography: p.
   1. Bible. O. T.—Dictionaries. I. Bruce, Freder-
ick Fyvie, 1910-   II. Title.
BS440.V75   1978   221.3   78-7564
ISBN 0-8007-0930-6

CONTENTS

PUBLISHER'S FOREWORD

The first edition of W. E. Vine's *An Expository Dictionary of New Testament Words* was published in the United Kingdom in 1940, and many thousands of biblical scholars have studied the Scriptures using this valuable tool. It is a classic in the study of sacred literature, and has been published in various countries throughout the world; yet very little is known about the compiler of this great work—other than his life span: 1873–1949.

An Expository Dictionary of New Testament Words is probably his best-known work, and his status as a Greek scholar is unsurpassed, but William Edwy Vine contributed many valuable writings in his lifetime. Some of his other published works are: *A Greek Testament Grammar; A Commentary on the Epistle to the Romans; The Roman Empire in Prophecy; The Divine Inspiration of the Bible; John: His Record of Christ; The Church and the Churches; Isaiah: Prophecies, Promises, Warnings.*

The editor of this previously unpublished manuscript, F. F. Bruce, is far better known to modern Bible scholars. Born in 1910 in Scotland, he was educated at the University of Aberdeen, the University of Cambridge, and the University of Vienna. He now makes his home in Buxton, Derbyshire, England, where he is the Rylands Professor of Biblical Criticism and Exegesis at the University of Manchester, England. His list of published

7

works includes *The Books and the Parchments; New Testament History; Second Thoughts on the Dead Sea Scrolls; The English Bible; The Epistles of John; The Defense of the Gospel in the New Testament.*

The general style of W. E. Vine's *An Expository Dictionary of New Testament Words* has been followed in the editing of this companion volume of Old Testament Words. Instead of A.V. (Authorized Version) referred to in the earlier volume, KJV (the King James Version, published 1611) is referred to. R.V. (Revised Version, published 1881–1885) is also quoted here. The reader will recognize American spellings rather than the Anglicized words of the author's New Testament dictionary.

Also included in this first-time publication of Hebrew word meanings is an Appendix developed from *When, How, and by Whom Was the Bible Written* by Rev. James Todd, D.D.; a Chart of Historical Comparisons prepared by Dr. John A. Cawood of Philadelphia College of Bible, showing the time span of the Old and New Testaments; and a comprehensive bibliography by Dr. David Huttar of Nyack College (N.Y.) complete the volume.

This material will help provide much-needed background for Bible scholars, seminary and Bible college students whose knowledge of the Old Testament may be limited. It is through the study of the Old Testament that we can appreciate the many truths found in the New. The beauty of Vine's language in describing the symbolism of the various Hebrew terms, as well as his scholarly knowledge of the Scriptures, make this—his final legacy—a worthy contribution of one who devoted a lifetime to the study of God's Word.

THE PUBLISHERS

INTRODUCTION

This expository dictionary carries Old Testament words not previously published in the format done so well by W. E. Vine in his original work. When Mr. Vine's *Expository Dictionary of New Testament Words* had been finally seen through the press, he turned his attention to a similar project on Old Testament words. He made no claim to the kind of expert mastery of Hebrew that he had of Greek, but he had been for many years a careful student of the Hebrew Bible. At the time of his death in November, 1949, he left in manuscript the material contained here. The words which are treated in this edition are, for the most part, words of theological importance, but the list includes some technical terms and other words of general interest. Readers who have profited by Mr. Vine's Greek word studies will be glad to have this selection of word studies in the Old Testament.

F. F. BRUCE

An Expository Dictionary
of
Old Testament Words

OLD TESTAMENT
WORD MEANINGS

A

ABIB

This was the first month of the Jewish year (corresponding to March–April); it was made the first month to commemorate the deliverance from Egypt (Exodus 9:31; 12:2; 13:4; 34:18). The word *'abîb* is a collective noun and signifies "ears of corn." In that month the Passover feast occurred and on the second day the sheaf of the firstfruits of the harvest was waved (Leviticus 23:10–12). God promised His people latter rain (necessary for the "ears of corn") in that month, the floors would be full of wheat, and the vats overflowing with wine and oil (Joel 2:23, 24). After the Babylonian exile it was more commonly called Nisan.

ABOMINATION

This word has several meanings in the Old Testament, and it is used to translate four Hebrew words. It is frequently used to express the idea of something loathed, especially religiously. To eat food with Hebrews was an abomination to the Egyptians (Genesis 43:32). Their exclusiveness extended this to all foreigners who had no regard for their scruples. That is the sense of the word in Exodus 8:26 (the cow was held sacred by all the Egyptians). The calling of a shepherd was "an abomination unto the Egyptians" (Genesis 46:34), that is, it was looked upon with intense hatred. In Leviticus 18:22 it signifies an object of divine abhorrence. In Ezekiel 22:11 it denotes a detestable deed. In all these references the same Hebrew word *tô'ēbhāh* is used. "Abomination" is used for an actual idol when the Hebrew word is not always the same in each instance, for example, 2 Kings 23:13. Idols are also referred to in Isaiah 44:19 and Deuteronomy 32:16 (plural). The word is used sometimes as a technical term for stale sacrificial flesh which has not been eaten within the prescribed time (Leviticus 7:18). Leviticus 19:7 and Ezekiel 4:14 have a bearing on this. In some passages it is used for the flesh of prohibited animals, as in Isaiah 66:17 and Ezekiel 8:9, 10, or it refers to objects connected with idolatry and especially of heathen deities, for example, Hosea 9:10. In Daniel 12:11 "the abomination (Hebrew *shiqqûṣ*) that maketh desolate" is the idolatrous installation to be set up in the Jerusalem Temple by "the prince that shall come" (Daniel 9:26), which will bring the desolation of the end-time, when the covenant made by him is broken. See Daniel 8:11–14; 9:27; and Matthew 24:15.

ADAMANT

This is used of an especially hard stone such as the emery stone or a form of corundum which is the hardest substance known with the exception of diamonds. (The word "diamond" is a corruption of the word "adamant.") The word illustrates hardheartedness in resisting the truth of God (Zechariah 7:12; compare Jeremiah 17:1).

In Ezekiel 3:8, 9 it illustrates the divine firmness imparted to Ezekiel in resisting the Israelites who refused to listen to the voice of God. He says, "Behold, I have made thy face strong against their faces, and thy forehead strong against their foreheads. As an adamant harder than flint have I made thy forehead."

ADJURATION

The primitive meaning of the word "adjure" is to put under an oath, as in Joshua 6:26. A judge or king, or high priest with official authority put a person on his solemn oath, involving the obligation of witnesses; Saul adjured the people not to eat till the evening (1 Samuel 14:24). But the word is used in the sense of making a solemn charge without the accompaniment of an oath, as when Ahab adjured Micaiah to tell the truth (1 Kings 22:16; compare with Song of Solomon 2:7 R.V.; 3:5; 5:8, 9; 8:4). In Leviticus 5:1, anyone who heard the voice of adjuration and was a witness of it, even though he had only known about it, had to bear his iniquity if he did not utter it.

When the high priest adjured the Lord Jesus by the living God to tell the truth as to whether He was the Christ the Son of God, though He had refused to reply to false witnesses, He answered the adjuration by an affirmative, thus declaring His own Godhead (compare Mark 5:7; Acts 19:13; 1 Thessalonians 5:27).

ADOPTION

This means to take care of a son who was not one by birth. Abraham adopted Eliezer; Pharaoh's daughter adopted Moses; Mordecai adopted Esther. See also the instances of Sarai in relation to the son to be borne by Hagar; and Leah and Rachel in relation to the children to be born of Zilpah and Bilhah. The act described in Genesis 30:3 represented the entire appropriation of the sons as equal in rights to those by the legitimate wife. Jacob adopted Joseph's two sons, Ephraim and Manasseh, putting them on the same footing as his two elder sons Reuben and Simeon (Genesis 48:5).

AFFINITY

In the Old Testament this word is used, not in the sense of relationship by marriage but of an evil association on the part of God's people with the ungodly. In 1 Kings 3:1 it is recorded that Solomon made affinity with Pharaoh. Jehoshaphat did so with Ahab (2 Chronicles 18:1). It was a grievous thing in Ezra's eyes that God's people were joining in affinity with the peoples of the land that were practicing abomination (Ezra 9:14).

ALMUG

This wood (1 Kings 10:11, 12) is thought to be a kind of sandalwood. The inferior spelling "algum" is found in 2 Chronicles 2:8. It was brought specially from Ophir and Lebanon. Primarily the almug tree came from Ophir, an Arabian town by the Red Sea, and was brought to Tyre by Hiram's merchant fleet. Accordingly, trees would come with the firs and cedars from Lebanon and all three would be described collectively as "out of Lebanon" (2 Chronicles 2:8). The wood was used for pillars and stairs in the temple and in the king's house, and for harps and psalteries.

ANAKIM

The Anakim (literally, "long-necked") are first mentioned as such in Deuteronomy 1:28. They were a race of giants (2:10, 11 R.V.), "Rephaim," a word used to de-

scribe the early giant peoples of Palestine. In Numbers
13:33 R.V. they are spoken of as "the Nephilim, the sons
of Anak, which come of the Nephilim." Anak is thus
regarded as the ancestor. The word "Anak," however,
may be the name of the race rather than of an individual.
This is indicated by the use of the article with the words
("the Anak") in the original in Numbers 13:22, 28;
Joshua 15:13, 14; 21:11; Judges 1:20. The greatest man
among them was Arba, who gave his name to the city
Kiriath-arba, Joshua 14:15, called Hebron, Genesis 23:2;
35:27. Arba seems to have been the progenitor of the
race; presumably he founded the city seven years before
the Egyptian Zoan (Numbers 13:22).

The Anakim were a terror to the spies (Numbers
13:28), but were chiefly destroyed by Joshua, except a
remnant who escaped to Philistine cities (Joshua 11:21,
22). Caleb ultimately destroyed them (15:14).

The Nephilim mentioned above are found in two passages, in Genesis 6:4 R.V. which indicates the existence
of giants born in a manner contrary to nature (the word
may be derived from the Hebrew verb *nāphal*, to fall).
These perished in the Flood with the rest of the race
(except for Noah's family), Genesis 7:21–23. The other
passage, Numbers 13:33 R.V., indicates a similar kind of
being identical with the Anakim. These are to be distinguished from those before the Flood. The records of the
Canaanite nations suggest, however, that the existence
of these beings indicates similar conditions contrary to
nature, and not merely a race of formidable persons of
gigantic stature.

ANKLET

Ankle rings were worn by women on both feet, joined
by short chains, which "made a tinkling" as they walked,

and caused them to take short, graceful steps. These were an accompaniment of the godless conduct of certain of "the daughters of Zion," against whom Jehovah spoke through Isaiah (Isaiah 3:16).

ANOINT, ANOINTED

To put oil on the head or body was a general custom in the east (for example, Ruth 3:3). To cease anointing was a sign of mourning (2 Samuel 14:2; Daniel 10:3). It was a token of respect to a guest, the omission of which was a failure in the matter of hospitality (see Luke 7:46). Metaphorically, to be anointed with oil expressed spiritual joy and refreshment (Psalms 23:5; 45:7; 92:10; Isaiah 61:3).

The sacred use of oil was for anointing things or persons in consecrating them to God, as when Jacob anointed the pillar which he had used as a stone for resting his head (Genesis 28:18). Anointing was a symbol of the qualifications divinely imparted in the consecration of persons for the discharge of their office, whether prophets (1 Kings 19:16; see *Expository Dictionary of New Testament Words* under the words "ANOINT, ANOINTING"); priests (Leviticus 4:3, first, priests in general, subsequently only the high priest), or kings (1 Samuel 10:1). The priest and the king (or civil ruler) are associated as "the two sons of oil" (KJV "anointed ones") in Zechariah 4:14. David was anointed three times in connection with his kingship, first, prospectively, 1 Samuel 16:13; then as king over Judah, 2 Samuel 2:4; then over all Israel, 5:3. "The LORD's anointed" was the phrase used to designate the king chosen by God (1 Samuel 12:3; Lamentations 4:20). Christ is twice so designated, as the Messiah (Psalms 2:2; Daniel 9:25, 26; R.V. "the anointed one"). Christ combines all three offices in His own Person.

In Isaiah 10:27, the yoke of Assyrian tyranny was to be destroyed "because of the anointing," that is, because of the consecration divinely appointed for God's people Israel, by reason of their union with their king "The LORD's anointed." Their deliverance is due to identification with him.

With all this sacred anointing the Holy Spirit and His ministry are inseparably associated, as is shown in passages in the New Testament; compare Acts 10:38; 2 Corinthians 1:21; 1 John 2:20, 27.

APPLE OF THE EYE

This phrase is used in a prayer, in Psalms 17:8; as a promise in Zechariah 2:8; as a fulfilled act in Deuteronomy 32:10; in an exhortation, Proverbs 7:2. The "apple" is the most precious and most securely guarded part of the eye. It feels most intensely the least injury; the loss of it is irreparable. The Hebrew word in this phrase is 'îshôn, literally, "the little man," so called because of the image on the retina.

ARMLETS

This is the R.V. word for the KJV "tablets" in Exodus 35:22 and Numbers 31:50. The armlet was a flat open clasp worn on the upper part of the arm. It is mentioned in the list of votive offerings for the Tabernacle (Exodus 35) and as part of the offerings to the Lord from the spoil taken from the Midianites (Numbers 31:50). Compare 2 Samuel 1:10, "bracelet."

ARMOURY

There was an armoury, for storing arms, at the northwest corner of "the city of David," mentioned as "the turning of the wall" in Nehemiah 3:19, literally, "the armoury of the corner." David built a tower for an armoury which held "a thousand bucklers [or shields]" (Song of Solomon 4:4). A comparison of 1 Kings 7:2 with Isaiah 22:8 suggests that Solomon's "house of the forest of Lebanon" may have served as an armoury. The word is used metaphorically in the description of God's judgments upon Babylon in Jeremiah 50:25: "The LORD hath opened his armoury, and hath brought forth the weapons of his indignation."

ARROGANT, ARROGANCE, ARROGANCY, ARROGANTLY

Arrogance as overbearing conceit, or the boastful assertion of more than one has a right to, is a rendering used only four times in KJV, in Samuel 2:3; Proverbs 8:13; Isaiah 13:11; Jeremiah 48:29. R.V. uses it there as well as in 2 Kings 19:28 (KJV "tumult"); Isaiah 16:6 (KJV "haughtiness"); 37:29 (KJV "tumult"). The words "arrogant" and "arrogantly" are the R.V. renderings for the KJV "fools" and "foolishly" in Psalms 75:4, and for the KJV "hard things," in Psalms 94:4.

ASHES

"Sackcloth and ashes" are the tokens of humiliation and penitence, usually accompanied by fasting (for example, Job 42:6; Esther 4:1; Isaiah 58:5; 61:3; Daniel 9:3; Jonah 3:6; Matthew 11:21). Ashes, with dust or earth were also a sign of mourning (compare Job 2:8; 12). Ashes on the head were a token of physical humiliation and disgrace (2 Samuel 13:19). In some places they are a synonym of "worthlessness" and "insignificance" (Genesis 18:27; in Job 13:12 R.V. "your memorable sayings are proverbs of ashes," that is, "trashy proverbs"; 30:19; Isaiah 44:20).

The ashes of a red heifer, with those of cedarwood, hyssop, and scarlet, were used for the preparation of the water of separation (Numbers 19:9, 10).

A special term (*deshen*) is used for the ashes of the animals burnt in sacrifice (Leviticus 1:16; 4:12; 6:10, 11). The corresponding Hebrew verb signifies the clearing away of the ashes of the sacrifice (in Exodus 27:3 R.V. "take away" for KJV "receive"; in Numbers 4:13 "take away").

In Exodus 9:8, 10 the ashes of the furnace translates a different word (Hebrew *pîaḥ*) found only here and probably denoting "soot" (R.V. margin).

In 1 Kings 20:38, 41 the KJV confuses the word *'ēpher* (ashes) with *'aphēr*, a bandage or "headband" (R.V.).

ASSAY, ASSAYED

The word so rendered signifies more than merely to attempt to do a thing; it means to set oneself to do. So in Deuteronomy 4:34, "Hath God assayed to go and take him a nation?"; in 1 Samuel 17:39, "David girded his sword upon his apparel [R.V., for KJV "armour"] and he assayed to go" (more than "attempted"); in Job 4:2, "If we assay to commune with thee."

The Greek verb in the New Testament means to try. See *Expository Dictionary of New Testament Words* under "TRY, TRIED."

For ASSEMBLY see CONGREGATION

ASSURANCE

In Isaiah 32:17 R.V. has "quietness and confidence" for KJV "quietness and assurance." The original word signifies to hang upon something, and accordingly the meaning is "trust." See *Expository Dictionary of New Testament Words,* pages 84, 85.

ATONEMENT, DAY OF

There are two special passages relating to this annual fast of the people of Israel, Leviticus 16 and 23:26–32. Additional particulars are given in Exodus 30:10 and Numbers 29:7–11 (compare Leviticus 25:9). Leviticus 16:3–10 describes the general ceremonial; 11–34 gives the details; Numbers 29:7–11 describes the victims; Leviticus 23:26–32 delineates how the people were to act.

It signifies the day of expiation (or propitiation), that is, the day on which the high priest offered (at his own cost) a bullock for a sin offering and a ram for a burnt offering; and he offered (at the public cost) for himself and his priestly family, two additional goats and another ram for a burnt offering. They were an offering for the people. The one goat "for Jehovah" was sacrificed as a sin offering and its blood sprinkled on (that is, in the front of) the mercy seat (as with the bullocks). The other goat was "for Azazel," the scapegoat. On his head the high priest laid his hands, confessing over it the sins of the people. Then this goat was led by a chosen man into the wilderness (a land uninhabited) and there let loose. These goats have been held to typify: the slain one, the atoning and vicarious sacrifice of Christ in bearing "our sins in his own body on the tree" (1 Peter 2:24). The freed one typifies the complete removal of our sin out of sight. The rendering in Leviticus 16:10, 26 should be "the goat for complete sending away" (not "the goat for the scapegoat")—from the root *'āzal,* to remove completely.

On that day, and that day only, the high priest entered

four times into the holy of holies, spoken of as "once" in Hebrews 9:7.

This day was appointed as a day of national humiliation, a day of affliction, a sabbath, a day of rest, but not like other sabbaths—days of joy—for on this day the sin of the nation was brought to remembrance. The day was the tenth of Tishri the seventh month (corresponding to September–October), five days before the Feast of Tabernacles. The command to the people to afflict their souls involved strict abstinence from food and drink, thus indicating their self-humiliation in the sight of God.

AWL

The boring of a slave's ear with an awl signified his volunteering perpetual service when he might be free at the year of release (Exodus 21:6; Deuteronomy 15:17). This is quite distinct from what is set forth in the Hebrew of Psalms 40:6, which reads "ears hast thou digged for me" (the Septuagint version, quoted in Hebrews 10:5, "a body hast thou prepared for me"). In the Exodus passage the idea is that of binding under a lasting obligation to render service. "Ears hast thou digged" suggests the impartation of the physical faculty by means of which the capacity of fulfilling the will of another would be exercised, and "a body hast thou prepared for me" is just another way of expressing the same thought. The impartation of ears to hear implies the existence of a body by which the instruction received through the ears (plural, not the boring of an ear) is carried out.

The body prepared by the Father for the Son was the instrument of His self-surrender and His entire and devoted submission to the Father's will. The Son Himself, in partaking of flesh and blood, put Himself into the position for rendering perfect obedience to Him.

B

For BACA see WEEPING

BAG

A bag was a shepherd's wallet, or a scrip for a journey made of a kid's skin with a strap fastened to each end so as to hang from the shoulder. It was used for carrying food, and was an emblem of a pilgrim or pastoral life. David put the pebbles in one when he went to meet Goliath (1 Samuel 17:40, Hebrew, *kelî*).

Another kind of bag was used for carrying a merchant's weights. The materials used varied. The warning against false weights (Deuteronomy 25:13; Proverbs 20:23, Hebrew, *kîs*) arose from the practice of putting pebbles and pieces of metal into such a bag so as to make an evil gain by cheating the purchaser.

A bag was used as a purse for money (Proverbs 1:14, "purse"). The way in which this word is used in Isaiah 46:6 is suggestive of extravagant waste. See *Expository Dictionary of New Testament Words*, under the word "BAG."

Another word signifying a satchel, is found in 2 Kings 5:23, Hebrew, *ḥārîṭ*, plural *'ḥarîṭîm*, of the bag into which Naaman's gift was put. The same word is used in Isaiah 3:22 (R.V. "satchels," for KJV "crisping pins"); it was an ornamentally woven sort of pouch.

Another word signifying something tied, either round about like a parcel or at the neck like a pouch is Hebrew *serōr.* Sometimes the tying material was fastened with a seal. Job likens his irrevocable past to a bag, or purse, with a seal on its string (Job 14:17). Natural prosperity, unblessed by God, is described in Haggai 1:6 as money in a bag with holes. The same word is used of a purse that was found in the sacks of Joseph's brothers (Genesis 42:35). Compare Luke 12:33; 22:35; John 12:6. See also "girdle," Matthew 10:9; Mark 6:8 (margin); Acts 21:11.

BALANCE

This (besides its literal use) is used metaphorically as an emblem of justice (Job 31:6), or as the test of uprightness and truth (Psalms 62:9; Proverbs 11:1), literally, "a balance of deceit" (margin).

BALDNESS, BALD HEAD

Baldness was sometimes a mark of leprosy (Leviticus 13:40–42); a humiliation to captives (Deuteronomy 21:11, 12; Isaiah 3:24); a mark of mourning (Isaiah 15:2; Jeremiah 16:6; 47:5; Ezekiel 7:18). Priests were forbidden to "make baldness" on their heads (Leviticus 21:5). The Israelites were forbidden to make baldness between their eyes as mourners, because they were "an holy people unto the LORD thy God" (Deuteronomy 14:1, 2).

Egyptians, on the contrary, shaved on joyous occasions, letting the hair grow in mourning. Joseph had to follow the customs of the Egyptians on this occasion (see Genesis 41:14).

Artificial baldness marked the termination of the vow of a Nazirite and testified to purification (Numbers 6:9; Acts 18:18; 21:24).

Among Israelites baldness was rare, hence it became

an object of derision. When the young men mocked Elisha, calling him a bald head and telling him to go up (2 Kings 2:23), they suggested that he was too old for this world, and should go up to heaven as his master had done. This was a taunt, as baldness was a mark of leprosy and humiliation.

BALM

The word is a shortened form of "balsam." The substances which are mentioned with it in Genesis 37:25 indicate that it was an aromatic or spice. The balm of Gilead, there mentioned, was famed as among the best products of Canaan (compare Genesis 43:11). It was exported to Egypt, and to Tyre (Ezekiel 27:17). It had medicinal properties. Jeremiah, speaking figuratively and lamenting the spiritual condition of his people says, "Is there no balm in Gilead; is there no physician there?" The balm is a symbol of spiritual healing for the spiritual disease of Israel (Jeremiah 8:22; see also 46:11; 51:8). The tree from which the product was taken by incisions was cultivated near Jericho, and grew to about fourteen feet high. The incisions yield three or four drops a day. The product is named *balasān* in Arabic, hence probably Hebrew *bōsem* and our word balsam.

BAND

There are three meanings to this word as in the English versions:

1. Anything that binds, whether for restrictive purposes or for strengthening. The following are the Hebrew words connected with this significance.

(a) *'abhōth*, something twined or twisted: Job 39:10, "Canst thou bind the unicorn with his band?"; translated "ropes" in R.V. Judges 15:13, 14 (KJV "cords"); "cords" in Psalms 2:3 (for the word "bands" in that verse, see *f* below); 118:27; 129:4; "wreathen work" in Exodus 28:14, 22, 24, 25; 39:15, 17, 18; "bands" in Ezekiel 3:25; 4:8; Hosea 11:4, "I drew them . . . with bands of love."

(*b*) *'ēsûr*, anything that will bind, whether a flaxen rope (Judges 15:14, of Samson's bands; Ecclesiastes 7:26, of the snares of an evil woman), or a fetter of iron or brass (Daniel 4:15, 23).

(*c*) *ḥebhel*, a rope or cord, whether for fastening tents (Isaiah 33:20), or as the "tacklings" on board ship (Isaiah 33:23), especially for measuring—a measuring "line" (2 Samuel 8:2; Psalms 78:55 and so forth). In Psalms 119:61 R.V. "the cords of the wicked [KJV bands] ensnare me" (see the KJV margin—"companies" is probably the meaning). In Zechariah 11:7, 14 "Bands" is the name of one of the two staves, representing the brotherhood between Judah and Israel; the other, "Beauty," representing the covenant made with the people. In Esther 1:6; Job 41:1; and Ezekiel 27:24 it is used of "cords" for binding.

(*d*) *ḥarṣubbāh* signifies fetters, as of the pangs in the death of the wicked (Psalms 73:4, "bands"; R.V. margin, "pangs"); in R.V. Isaiah 58:6, of the fast that pleases God, namely, "to loose the bonds [KJV "bands"] of wickedness."

(*e*) *môsēr* is properly something for chastising; hence a bond for curbing, Job 39:5; Psalms 2:3; 107:14; Isaiah 28:22; 52:2; Jeremiah 2:20; 5:5; 27:2; 30:8.

(*f*) *môshekheth* is a rope to draw with; this word is found only in Job 38:31, "Canst thou . . . loose the bands of Orion?"; that is, "Hast thou got strength enough" to free those unseen hindrances exerted in nature in connection with the stars spoken of as Orion.

Only Christ will do this being Himself the Creator of these orbs.

Note: The word *môṭāh* denotes the pole or chief part of the yoke that binds oxen together. In the two passages where this word occurs, Leviticus 26:13 and Ezekiel 34:27 the R.V. rightly renders the word "bars" for KJV "bands."

2. The word *sāphah*, a band (literally, "lip"), is used to signify a ribbon. There was a hole in the midst of the robe of the ephod with a band round about the hole to prevent its being rent, Exodus 39:23 (R.V. a "binding"). Another word, *ḥēshebh*, is used in connection with the ephod in Exodus 28:8, 27, 28; 29:5; 39:5, 20, 21; Leviticus 8:7, where R.V. has "the cunningly woven band" for the KJV "curious girdle."

3. The word "band" is also used to signify a troop or company. The following Hebrew words are thus translated.

(a) *'agaph* which means originally the wing of an army. R.V. renders it "bands" in Ezekiel 12:14; 17:21, as in KJV but renders it "hordes" in Ezekiel 38:6, 9, 22; 39:4.

(b) *gedhûdh* is a noun from a verb meaning to penetrate, and this signifies a band invading a country; it is used in 2 Samuel 4:2; 1 Kings 11:24 (R.V. "troop"); 2 Kings 6:23; 13:20, 21; 24:2 and corresponding passages in Chronicles.

(c) *ḥayil* denotes strength; hence a strong army, a force, 1 Samuel 10:26 (R.V. the "host"); Ezra 8:22.

(d) *ḥōṣēṣ*, a word signifying to divide and hence divided into companies. This is found only in Proverbs 30:27, speaking of locusts which without a king go forth by "bands."

(e) *maḥaneh* signifies a camp but in Genesis 32:7 and 10 the KJV renders it "bands," the R.V. "companies."

(f) *rō'sh* denotes a head: it is found in the sense of "band" only in 1 Chronicles 12:23 (R.V. "heads") and Job 1:17, "the Chaldeans made three bands."

BANNER

1. Hebrew *nēs* may literally mean either "that which shines" or "that which is lifted up"; it is used of the banner given by God to them that fear Him (Psalms 60:4); in Isaiah 13:2 (KJV "banner," R.V. "ensign" as in 5:26; 11:10; 30:17; 49:22). Moses called the altar of thanksgiving, after the defeat of Amalek "Jehovah-nissi" (Jehovah, my banner), Exodus 17:15; the altar was thus a covenant pledge that Jehovah would enable His people to defeat Amalek and all their foes. The banner was a rallying point to kindle hope and efforts, a signal raised on a special occasion, and always on some elevated place or object. The word is used of the "standard" (KJV "pole") upon which Moses put the brazen serpent (Numbers 2:8, 9).

2. The *degel* is a military standard; it signifies that which is meant to be seen. It is used of the standards of the tribes of Israel in the wilderness (Numbers 2:2). Also in Psalms 20:5, "In the name of our God will we set up our banners"; in Song of Solomon 6:4, 10 the Shulammite, with a beauty that overcomes the beholder, is compared to "an army with banners."

BANQUET, BANQUETING

1. Hebrew *mishteh* denotes a drinking and is used in Esther 5:4; 6:14; 7:2, 7, 8; Daniel 5:10. It is derived from

the verb *shāthāh,* "to drink," Esther 7:1: "So the king and Haman came to banquet" (literally, "to drink").

2. Hebrew *yayin* denotes wine; in Song of Solomon 2:4, "He brought me to the banqueting house" is literally "the house of wine." Note: In Job 41:6, for the KJV "Shall the companions make a banquet of him?" R.V. has "make traffic of him" (the Hebrew *kārāh* means to bargain). In Amos 6:7, for "the banquet of them that stretched themselves" R.V. has "the revelry" (Hebrew *mirzēah* is used as yells of joy).

BASE

This word is used figuratively to signify low in the social scale, of lowly birth or station; then, humble or unassuming. In Isaiah 3:5, "the base against the honourable" means the low-born against the nobles. In Daniel 4:17 "the basest of men" does not mean the vilest, but one who is of a lowly position (R.V. "lowest"). So David's word to Michal, "I . . . will be base in mine own sight" (2 Samuel 6:22). In Malachi 2:9 it signifies ignoble; also in Ezekiel 17:14; 29:14, 15. In Job 30:8, "children of base men" is literally "sons [or men] of no name," that is, sons of one who has no name, the ignoble.

It is also used of those who are morally low. Thus in Deuteronomy 13:13, R.V. has "Certain base fellows are gone out" for KJV "Certain men, the children of Belial," literally, "men, sons of worthlessness." Compare 1 Samuel 1:16.

Note: A base, signifying that on which something stands, or on which one steps, has no connection with the preceding word. See, for example, 1 Kings 7:34, 35; in verse 31 R.V. "pedestal." In Ezekiel 43:13 a different word is rendered "base" in R.V., where the meaning

is the elevated part (of the altar; margin "back"; KJV
"higher place").

BASKET

This translates five different Hebrew words:

1. *sal*, a bag of interwoven twigs. Pharaoh's chief
baker dreamt he carried three on his head (Genesis
40:16–18). These were baskets of white bread (R.V.), not
white baskets (KJV). Such baskets were used to carry the
unleavened bread, oiled cakes and wafers for the offering of the consecration of the priests (Exodus 29:3–23;
Leviticus 8:2–26); hence in Leviticus 8:31 it is called
"the basket of consecrations." They were used for the
Nazirite's offering (Numbers 6:15–19). Gideon carried
his provision for the angel in such a basket (Judges 6:19).

2. *salsillôth* is so translated in Jeremiah 6:9, "as a
grape-gatherer into the baskets" (or "grape-gatherer's
baskets"). Some translators suggest "upon the shoots,"
the idea being the gleaning of an already stripped vine
(see the first part of the verse concerning the remnant).

3. *tene'* is a basket for ordinary household or agricul-
tural use; the firstfruits were carried in it (Deuteronomy
26:2–4). The blessing of the basket and the store (or
kneading trough), emblematic of national prosperity,
was assured by God as a result of good deeds
(Deuteronomy 28:5). The opposite condition would
meet with God's curse (Deuteronomy 28:17).

4. The *dûdh* was a large tapering basket; it was used
for carrying clay to the brick kilns, either carried on the
back or borne, two at a time, on a pole or yoke between
two men. Israel was delivered from these burdens in
Egypt when God set them free: they are mentioned in
Psalms 81:6 R.V. "his hands were freed from the basket"

(not "pots," as in KJV). In this kind of basket the heads of Ahab's sons were sent to Jehu in Jezreel (2 Kings 10:7). The word is translated "kettle" in 1 Samuel 2:14 and "pot" in Job 41:20.

5. The word *kelûbh* is used in Amos 8:1, 2 for a basket of summer fruits. In Jeremiah 5:27 it signifies a bird cage, probably made of basketwork.

For BASON (BASIN) see BOWL

BATH, BATHE

Washing or bathing was enjoined by the Law for purification from uncleanness of any kind, such as leprosy (Leviticus 22:6; see also 15:5; Numbers 19:7, 19; 2 Samuel 11:2, 4; 2 Kings 5:10). The high priest bathed himself on the Day of Atonement before each act of expiation (Leviticus 16:4, 24); also at his consecration (8:6).

Instances of bathing in a river are recorded in the case of Pharaoh's daughter (Exodus 2:5 R.V.); compare 2 Kings 5:14, "dipped." In several passages the word *rāḥaṣ* means to wash (not bathe) and this is the rendering usually adopted.

BEAST

Three different words are so rendered:

1. The Hebrew word *behēmāh* is used to denote any quadruped. It is set in contradistinction to man (Genesis 6:7; Exodus 9:9, 10, 25); it is used of clean beasts (Genesis 7:2); of animals to be eaten (Leviticus 11:2); as one of the four chief classes of vertebrates—beasts, fowls, creeping things, fishes (1 Kings 4:33); of domestic animals (1 Kings 18:5; Nehemiah 2:12); of wild animals (Deuteronomy 32:24). It is inappropriately rendered

"cattle" in some passages (for example, Genesis 1:24–26; 2:20; Psalms 50:10).

2. Hebrew *be'îr* signifies beasts used as cattle or animals for other domestic purposes (Genesis 45:17; Exodus 22:5; Numbers 20:4, 8, 11): rendered "cattle" in some places: so in Psalms 78:48.

3. Hebrew *hayyāh* is used of animals in general (for example, Genesis 1:24; Leviticus 11:2); but of wild beasts, as distinct from Number 1, for example, Genesis 7:14; in Psalms 68:30 R.V. "the wild beast of the reeds"; "evil beast" in Genesis 37:20, 33; "beasts of the field" (Exodus 23:11); "ravenous beast" (Isaiah 35:9). This word is rendered "living creatures" in Ezekiel 1:5; "living thing" in Genesis 1:28; "life" in Psalms 143:3; Isaiah 57:10 (R.V. "quickening"); "appetite" in Job 38:39.

Note: The word *behēmôth* (which is found in Job 40:15; Psalms 73:22; Isaiah 30:6) is the plural of number 1. This is the animal mentioned in Job 40:15–24. It is almost certainly the hippopotamus. The rendering in verse 23 should be "he is confident though Jordan were poured into his mouth."

Symbolically, man in separation from God, and relying on his own thought and strength and resources, is as a beast. When Asaph envied the prosperity of the wicked, he confessed to God, "I was as a beast before thee" (Psalms 73:22); "man being in honour abideth not [that is, apart from God]: he is like the beasts that perish" (Psalms 49:12). The natural tendency of the beast is "downward" (Ecclesiastes 3:21). As man was made in the image of God, he is only manly when he is godly (compare 2 Peter 2:12). The four great successive empires which would govern Israel during "the times of the

Gentiles" are described as "four great beasts" (Daniel 7:3), coming up from the sea, that is, coming up from the confused condition of the nations.

BELIAL

There are two views as to the primary meaning of this word. The ordinary one is that it signifies worthlessness (from *belî-ya'al,* "no profit") or wickedness, and that the secondary meaning is destruction. Another view is that the primary meaning is the abode of the dead (either from *belî-ya'al,* no coming up, or from the root *bāla',* swallow up), hence, hopeless ruin, and the secondary meaning, extreme wickedness. In the Old Testament, the word, in the sense of "worthlessness" or "wickedness," is mostly used with another noun, for example, "daughter of Belial" (1 Samuel 1:16); "man" (1 Samuel 25:25; 2 Samuel 16:7; 20:1; Proverbs 16:27); "heart" (Deuteronomy 15:9, margin); "witness" (Proverbs 19:28); "person" (Proverbs 6:12; R.V. "worthless person"); "children" or "sons" (Deuteronomy 13:13 KJV; R.V. "base"; also in Judges 19:22; 20:13; 1 Samuel 2:12; 10:27; 25:17; 2 Samuel 23:6; 1 Kings 21:10, 13; 2 Chronicles 13:7); "men" (1 Samuel 30:22). The general meaning is thus "sinners of deepest dye."

In the sense of "destruction" the word is found five times: 2 Samuel 22:5; Psalms 18:4 R.V. "[floods of] ungodliness" (some render it "perdition"), in parallelism with "death" and "Sheol"; Psalms 41:8, "an evil disease"; Nahum 1:11 R.V. "[that counselled] wickedness" (some render it "hopeless ruin"); 1:15 R.V. "the wicked one" (or "the destroyer"). This meaning is borne out by the New Testament use of the word as a name of Satan (2 Corinthians 6:15).

BELOVED

This translates the word *dôdh* (probably connected with the name David), often used in Song of Solomon (as 1:13); elsewhere only in Isaiah 5:1, "a song of my beloved"; or *yādhîdh*, for example, Psalms 127:2, "he giveth his beloved sleep"; Isaiah 5:1 (twice) "my well-beloved" (compare Jedidiah, meaning "beloved of Jehovah," 2 Samuel 12:25). The related *yedhîdhûth*, "dearly beloved," is found only in Jeremiah 12:7, "the dearly beloved of my soul." Hebrew *mahamādh* occurs in Hosea 9:16, "the beloved fruit of their womb." In Daniel 9:23; 10:11, 19, *hamûdhôth*, literally, "desirable things," is used by God of Daniel; thus in 9:23, "thou art greatly beloved" signifies literally, "Thou art a precious treasure."

BESTEAD

This is found only in Isaiah 8:21; the word simply means placed. The words "hardly bestead" translate one Hebrew word, which the American R.V. translates "sore distressed": a good rendering is "hard pressed."

BEWRAY

This means to reveal, disclose (not connected with the word "betray"), Proverbs 29:24 (R.V. "uttereth [nothing]"). In Proverbs 27:16, a different word is used which the R.V. renders "encountereth"; margin "bewrayeth itself"; as in KJV, it means to light upon. In Isaiah 16:3 a different word is rendered "bewray not him that wandereth." It means to uncover, reveal (not "betray," as in the American R.V.). Compare Matthew 26:73.

BITTER, BITTERNESS

(*a*) This is used objectively, for example, cruel or bit-
ing words, as in Psalms 64:3, "bitter." It indicates the
misery of servitude, Exodus 1:14; the effects of impurity,
Proverbs 5:4; the misery of forsaking God, Jeremiah
2:19; of a life of sin, Jeremiah 4:18; the misfortunes of
bereavement, Ruth 1:20; Amos 8:10.

(*b*) It has a more subjective sense in describing such
emotions as sympathy in bereavement, Ruth 1:13 (margin), or the sorrow of childlessness, 1 Samuel 1:10; or
of misfortune, Ezekiel 27:31; or of disappointment,
Genesis 27:34; or a general feeling of wretchedness, Job
3:20. Such emotions find utterance in a "bitter cry," for
example, Genesis 27:34; Esther 4:1.

In this subjective sense it has the meaning of fierce-
ness of disposition, as in 2 Samuel 17:8, "chafed in their
minds," margin, "bitter of soul" ("as a bear robbed of her
whelps"); see also Habakkuk 1:6 "[the Chaldeans] that
bitter and hasty nation," that is, ready to take offense and
to act with impetuous fury. So Judges 18:25, "angry fellows" (margin, "bitter of soul").

(*c*) The word is used more figuratively of moral de-
pravity, as of the moral poison exhaled by the corrupt
Canaanites, Deuteronomy 32:32. Isaiah describes those
who would subvert the distinction between right and
wrong, as putting "bitter for sweet, and sweet for bitter"
(5:20).

(*d*) In Numbers 5:18, 19, 23, 24, 27, "the water of bit-
terness" (R.V.) is the water that causes the curse to be
fulfilled.

BLAST, BLASTED, BLASTING

This is used of (1) the blowing of a wind instrument,
Joshua 6:5; (2) the breath of Jehovah, Exodus 15:8; com-

pare Isaiah 30:28; 33:11 ("breath"); 37:7 (KJV "blast,"
R.V. "spirit"; so 2 Kings 19:7); (3) the tyranny of violent
nations, Isaiah 25:4; (4) a blowing that blights or curses,
2 Samuel 22:16; Psalms 18:15; Hebrew *neshāmāh;* Job
4:9, Hebrew *rûah;* "blasted" denotes "blighted,"
Genesis 41:6, 23, 27; 2 Kings 19:26; Isaiah 37:27; and
"blasting" (that is, "blight"), Deuteronomy 28:22; 1
Kings 8:37; 2 Chronicles 6:28; Amos 4:9; Haggai 2:17,
Hebrew *shādaph* and derivatives.

BOSSES

The word *gabbîm,* "bosses," used only in Job 15:26,
properly means things rounded, as of the back of an animal or the felloe of a wheel. Bucklers and shields were
made of layers of skin stretched over a frame, and a layer
of metal fixed over the whole. The word in Job 15 probably refers to this metal part. The rebel runs upon God
"with a stiff [that is, haughty] neck [R.V.], with [not
"upon" KJV] the thick bosses of his [the rebel's]
bucklers." A mad resistance! For "the shields of the
earth belong unto God" (Psalms 47:9).

BOTTLE

Bottles were of different kinds: the commonest kind
was a leathern bag made from the skin of an animal. The
smaller ones kept the shape of the animal with the legs
removed. The larger ones were sewn up. Those for hold-
ing water, milk, and so forth, usually had the hair left on,
but for wine and oil, the tanning had to be thoroughly
done; for this purpose acacia bark was used. During fer-
mentation the skin became distended. The Gibeonites
pretended that their bottles were rent because of their
long journey (Joshua 9:4, 13; compare Matthew 9:17).

Elihu compares his belly, from the effect of his spirit's filling him with words seeking utterance, to "wine which hath no vent; it is ready to burst like new bottles" (Job 32:19).

Hung in smoke to dry, the bottles become shriveled; so in Psalms 119:83 the psalmist says, "I am become like a bottle in the smoke."

Bottles of glass or potters' earthenware were easily broken. Through the rebellion of God's people against Him, He warned them that "every bottle shall be filled with wine," that is, that the inhabitants of Jerusalem and their rulers, would be made drunken with His judgments, and they would be dashed one against another (like bottles). They mocked at this (Jeremiah 13:12–14).

Jeremiah was told to buy a potter's earthen bottle and break it in the sight of the men that went with him, and declare that God would break the people and the city "as one breaketh a potter's vessel, that cannot be made whole again" (Jeremiah 19:1–11).

Clouds pouring down water are figuratively "the bottles of heaven" (Job 38:37). David says, "put thou my tears into thy bottle" (Psalms 56:8), that is, as a precious treasure to reserve them for a future recompense of joy.

BOWELS

This word is used (1) literally, of physical organs, as in 2 Chronicles 21:18, (2) figuratively, as the seat of deeply felt emotions: (a) indicating a thrill of affection or sympathy, Isaiah 16:11; 63:15; Song of Solomon 5:4 (KJV; R.V. "heart," margin, "bowels"); Jeremiah 31:20; compare Psalms 40:8; Hosea 11:8; (b) of distressing feelings, Job 30:27; Lamentations 1:20; 2:11.

BOWL

The Hebrew word *mizrāq*, denoting a large silver bowl, or basin, is mentioned several times in Numbers 7, where it was an offering of the princes of the congregation at the dedication of the Tabernacle. The word *gullāh* denotes a cruse or receptacle for oil, as in the lampstand of Zechariah's vision; see chapter 4:3. It is also used metaphorically of the lamp of life (Ecclesiastes 12:6).

Hebrew *sēphel* denotes a more primitive bowl which might be a hollow wooden dish to receive the milk of the flock and present it at the family meal (Judges 5:25). The same word is used in Judges 6:38. Other bowls were of earthenware.

BRANCH

This translates different Hebrew words. The following are the chief:

1. *zemôrāh*, the branch of a grapevine, Numbers 13:23; Isaiah 17:10, "slips"; Ezekiel 15:2; figuratively of Israel, Nahum 2:2. In Ezekiel 8:17, "they put the branch to their nose," describes primarily a ceremony connected with sun worship, but expresses the scorn of insolent security.

2. *yōneqeth*, literally a sucker, Job 14:7; it is used of the wicked, as a tree, Job 8:16; 15:30; of Israel under the figures of a vine, Psalms 80:11; a cedar, Ezekiel 17:22; an olive, Hosea 14:6.

3. *kippāh*, especially a palm branch, Job 15:32; in Isaiah 9:14 and 19:15, "palm branch (R.V.) and rush" are parallel to "head" and "tail" (verse 15), that is, the rulers and the rabble.

4. *nēṣer*, a small fresh green twig, Isaiah 11:1; 60:21;

Daniel 11:7; in Isaiah 14:19, it is used of the king of Babylon, where "an abominable branch" describes a useless shoot cut off and left to rot (compare John 15:16).

5. *ṣemaḥ,* shoot or sprout, or spring, as in Ezekiel 17:9; it is especially used of the Son of David, the Messiah, Jeremiah 23:5, "a righteous Branch"; 33:15, "a Branch of righteousness" (R.V.); Zechariah 3:8, "my servant the BRANCH"; 6:12, "the man whose name is The BRANCH." In Isaiah 4:2 "the branch of the LORD" is part of the fertility with which God will bless His land in the time of restoration. In Isaiah 61:11; Ezekiel 16:7; Hosea 8:7 *ṣemaḥ* is rendered "bud."

6. *qāneh* is frequently used of the branches of the golden lampstand in the Tabernacle (Exodus 25:36).

BRASS

In English this is an alloy consisting of copper and zinc. The brass of Scripture may probably be copper; this would appear to be referred to in Deuteronomy 8:9; Job 28:2 as the substance dug out of the earth. The word is used (*a*) of the actual metal, (*b*) symbolically. As to (*a*) the earliest record is in Genesis 4:22, where Tubal-cain is described as "an instructor of every artificer in brass and iron." In Exodus 38:2–8 the altar of burnt offering was overlaid with it, and the vessels of the altar, and the laver were made of it, as the emblem of strength and justice. In Numbers 21:9 the serpent made by Moses was of brass (that is, copper or bronze). In Deuteronomy 8:9 God describes Canaan to Israel as a land "out of whose hills thou mayest dig brass." In 1 Samuel 17:5 (compare 2 Samuel 8:8) Goliath's armor was of brass (bronze). For other Old Testament instances see 1 Kings 7:14; 2 Kings 25:13, 14; Jeremiah 52:17; 1 Chronicles 15:19; Job 28:2.

(See also Matthew 10:9; Revelation 9:20.) (*b*) Symbolically, brass speaks of (1) destructive heat and drought: "thy heaven that is over thy head shall be brass," Deuteronomy 28:23; (2) strength, resistance: "is my flesh of brass?" Job 6:12; "his [Behemoth's] bones are tubes of brass," 40:18 R.V.; compare 41:27; (3) power: "he hath broken the gates of brass," Psalms 107:16; compare Isaiah 45:2; Jeremiah 1:18; the third world empire, Daniel 2:32; (4) stubbornness: "thy neck is an iron sinew, and thy brow brass," Isaiah 48:4; compare Jeremiah 6:28; (5) poverty: "For brass I will bring gold," Isaiah 60:17; (6) plenty: "for wood brass" (60:17). The alloy brass, as we know it, may be denoted by Hebrew *hashmal* in Ezekiel 1:4 (KJV, R.V. "amber," R.V. margin, "electrum").

BREASTPLATE (of the high priest)

There are two significations attributed to the Hebrew word *hōshen* (Exodus 28:4, and so forth): either (1) the pocket or pouch of the oracle; or, (2) an ornament (from a root meaning to be beautiful). The breastplate was made of the same materials as the ephod. It was doubled forming a square, of a half cubit or span each way. It had four rows of precious stones, three in each row, each engraved with the name of a tribe of Israel. Into the breastplate were put the Urim and the Thummim ("lights and perfections"). The two golden rings were placed at the bottom inwards, and two were fastened to the ephod at the two top corners. A lace or ribbon of blue was passed through the two bottom rings. Two wreathen chains of gold were fastened through the upper rings to the ouches in which the onyx stones (on the right and left shoulders) were set and at their other ends to two rings at the top of the breastplate. Thus the ephod, onyx stones, and breastplate were all linked together.

Thus Israel was doubly represented before God, on the shoulders and on the heart, signifying strength and affection. All God's children are thus secured and loved. But the differing stones symbolize the fact that each believer reflects the glory of Christ according to the grace given him and to the measure in which he responds to it. So it will be hereafter.

As the breastplate, shoulder pieces and onyx stones were securely bound together, so believers are established, strengthened and settled in Christ. (See URIM and THUMMIM.)

BRIDE, BRIDEGROOM

In patriarchal times the bride was usually chosen by the parents or friends of the bridegroom and they would not necessarily consult him. Abraham sent a servant to find a bride for Isaac (Genesis 24). Judah chose Tamar for Er (38:6). Compare 21:21; 28:2; 2 Chronicles 24:3; 25:18. Where the bridegroom chose, the father sometimes made the proposal (Genesis 34:4–8; Judges 14:2, 10). Contrast Genesis 26:34, 35; 27:46, where the son chose a bride apart from the parents. The bride was often paid for, the father receiving money or service in return for his consent to part with her (Genesis 31:15; 34:12; 1 Samuel 18:25, 27). The bride received no dowry.

The main feature in the marriage ceremony was the fetching of the bride from her father's house to that of the bridegroom or that of his father.

At the appointed time the bridegroom set out with his companions (Judges 14:11) the sons of the bridechamber (Mark 2:19) with lights and music to fetch the bride. She also was accompanied by her companions, maidens, some of whom started with her from her father's house (Psalms 45:15), others joining the bridal party afterwards, all provided with lamps (Matthew 25:1–13). They went to meet the bridegroom, who conducted the whole party to the wedding feast. The bridegroom thus fetched the bride from her home to his.

A bridegroom was exempt from military service between betrothal and marriage (Deuteronomy 20:7) and for a year after marriage (24:5; compare Luke 14:20). The ceremony itself was more of a legal formality than a religious rite. The bride wore a veil, which quite covered her. "Attire" in Jeremiah 2:32 probably means the bridal sash (compare Isaiah 3:20 R.V. margin; 49:18). She remained veiled throughout. Weddings commonly took place in the evening. Hence Jacob did not detect the substitution of Leah for Rachel (Genesis 29:20–25). On the wedding day both bride and bridegroom wore a garland (crown) (Song of Solomon 3:11; compare Isaiah 61:10).

In spiritual symbolism in the Old Testament the bride is Israel and Jehovah is the bridegroom. See, for example, Psalms 45; Isaiah 54:5; 62:5; Jeremiah 3:14; Hosea 2:19. In the New Testament the Church is described as "the bride of Christ."

BUCKLER

Three forms of shield are mentioned: (1) the *ṣinnāh*, a large oblong shield, sometimes carried by a bearer (1 Samuel 17:7), sometimes used as a screen behind which a battering ram might be used against those who were defending a wall (Ezekiel 26:8, where the rendering should be "shall set up shields"). This is "the shield of faith" in Ephesians 6:16; (2) the *māgēn*, a small shield used by archers, for example, under Asa, in 2 Chronicles 14:8; (3) the *sōḥērāh*, mentioned only once in the Old Testament, in Psalms 91:4, "his truth is a shield and a buckler." Faith that is met by God's faithfulness makes the believer's defense perfect.

For BURDEN see ORACLE

BURNT OFFERING

The Hebrew word *'ōlāh* denotes that which ascends, that is, in smoke to God, being wholly reduced to ashes. While parts of every offering were burnt, this was a "whole burnt offering" (hence also called *kālîl*). It is first mentioned in Genesis 8:20, and is the one sacrifice in Genesis (15:9, 17; 22:2, 7, 8, 13). It was the highest gift of God and betokened the complete, unreserved consecration of the offerer, in his entire being, to God (Psalms 40:6–9). In certain passages the sin offering came first (Exodus 29:36–38; Leviticus 8:14, 18; 9:8, 12; 16:3, 5). Only when our sin is put away through the sacrifice of Christ can we present our bodies a living sacrifice. The burnt offering of any Israelite was to be offered "at the door of the tent of meeting," that it might be accepted before the Lord, and slain after he had laid his hands on its head, indicating that it was his representative; it was to be flayed and cut into pieces. Aaron's sons, the priests, were to put fire on the altar, lay the wood in order upon the fire and on this the pieces, the head and the fat, washing the inwards and the legs with water, and the whole was to be burnt on the altar, "an offering made by fire, of a sweet savour unto the LORD" (Leviticus 1:9; see also the remainder of the chapter). A meal offering ac-

companied it (Leviticus 9:16, 17), representing the sin-
lessness of Him who ever did God's will. For "the law of
the burnt offering" by the priests see 6:8–13. For the
burnt offering by Aaron, to make atonement for himself
and the people, see 9:7, 17.

There was a daily burnt offering, a lamb of the first
year, every morning and evening (Exodus 29:38–42); a
double one on the sabbath; an offering at the new moon
of the three great feasts, Passover, Pentecost and Tabernacles, on the great Day of Atonement and the Feast of
Trumpets; also private offerings at the consecration of a
priest (Exodus 29:15).

Vast numbers were offered at Solomon's dedication of
the Temple, but ordinarily they were divinely restricted,
to prevent the idea that man could buy God's favor with
costly gifts. Jephthah's vow was unwarranted by God
(Judges 11:30, 31).

On occasions of great solemnity the burnt offering was
offered without any other sacrifice, for example, after the
Flood, Genesis 8:20; or at a special revelation of God,
Genesis 22:13; Judges 13:16; or when entering on a
dangerous enterprise, Judges 6:23–26; or in a condition
of extremity through a powerful enemy, 1 Samuel 26:19.

C

CANDLE

Everywhere in the Bible "lamp" should be substituted for "candle." A candle is made of wax and finds no mention in Scripture. A lamp contains oil, a substance frequently conveying a spiritual meaning. It is used of the brevity of the prosperity of the wicked (Job 21:17, R.V. "lamp"). "The spirit of man is the lamp of the LORD" (Proverbs 20:27 R.V.), suggesting the power of the conscience. It has reference to the all-seeing power of the Lord to search out evildoers: "I will search Jerusalem with candles," Zephaniah 1:12 (KJV and R.V. but R.V. margin has Hebrew "lamps"). For the R.V. in other passages see, for example, Job 18:6; Psalms 18:28; Proverbs 24:20. See LAMP.

For CANDLESTICK see LAMPSTAND

CANKERWORM

The word *yeleq* denotes the licking locust (Joel 1:4). In Nahum 3:15, 16, the divine judgment on Nineveh forewarns the city that despite its efforts to multiply its numbers like the cankerworm, the other side of this illustration will be fulfilled; and as the cankerworm, after emerging from its caterpillar state, devours all vegetation before it, so the sword would devour the inhabitants. "The cankerworm spoileth, and flyeth away," is, literally, "spreadeth itself," that is, commits its depredations and then flies away.

CAPTAIN

This word translates several different Hebrew words: (1) *sar*, used especially of "the captain of the host" (Joshua 5:14, 15): military captains, for example, Genesis 26:26; it is also rendered "prince," for example, Exodus 2:14; "chief," Genesis 40:2; "keeper," Genesis 39:21; "ruler," Nehemiah 3:9; (2) *nāgîdh* signifies the foremost officer: it is used of the king, 1 Samuel 9:16 (R.V. "prince"); it is also rendered ruler, governor, noble; (3) *rō'sh*, a head (the usual meaning) rendered "captain" in Numbers 14:4; (4) *nāsî* literally means "lifted up," for example, Numbers 2:3, KJV (R.V. "prince" which is the usual meaning); *nāsî* and *rō'sh* occur together in Ezekiel 38:1, "chief prince"; (5) *qāsîn* means one who decides, Judges 11:6 (KJV "captain," R.V. "chief"), often rendered "prince"; (6) *tiphsār*, rendered captain (R.V. "marshall") in the two places where it is found, Jeremiah 51:27; Nahum 3:17; (7) *pehāh* (a loan word from Persian), usually a governor of a territory; "captains" in 1 Kings 20:24; "captains," 2 Kings 18:24; often rendered "governor," for example, Haggai 1:1 and so forth (margin, "captain"); (8) *rab*, commonly meaning much, many, great, is rendered "captain" in 2 Kings 25.

CASTLE

1. In the KJV of Genesis 25:16; Numbers 31:10; 1 Chronicles 6:54, the word *hāsēr* does not denote what is understood as a castle, but a circular group of tents, the encampment of a nomad tribe (R.V. "encampment").

2. Other words signifying a fortified tower or stronghold are rendered "castle" in 1 Chronicles 11:5, 7 KJV (R.V. "stronghold"); in the R.V. of 1 Kings 16:18 and 2 Kings 15:25, "castle" (for KJV "palace"). In Proverbs

18:19 the word rendered "citadel" signifies a fortress. The same word is used of palaces in Jeremiah 9:21; Hosea 8:14; Amos 2:2 and so forth. Many of the kings of Judah strengthened their dominions by fortifying cities with castles to protect the surrounding districts, 1 Chronicles 27:25; 2 Chronicles 17:12; 27:4. Such works were undertaken especially by David, Jehoshaphat, and Jotham.

In Nehemiah's time we read of a castle or citadel in Jerusalem apparently connected with the Temple (Nehemiah 2:8; 7:2, R.V. "castle," KJV "palace"). The Persian royal palace at Susa is called a castle, Hebrew, *bîrāh* (Nehemiah 1:1 R.V. margin). Compare Esther 1:2; and so forth (margin) and Daniel 8:2.

CAUL

This word has two meanings: (1) the fatty covering of the liver, which was to be burnt on the altar as an offering by fire to the Lord, Exodus 29:13, 22; Leviticus 3:4 and so forth. In Hosea 13:8 the rending of the caul of the heart by God signifies the utter destruction of evildoers, there said of His judgment upon Ephraim.

(2) The cauls mentioned in Isaiah 3:18 (R.V. margin "net works") were probably smallish head veils, worn over the brow and loosely fastened behind the neck under the hair. It was not considered proper to go to the door without them. They were fringed with embroidery and adorned with gold thread, small gilt discs.

CENSER

Two Hebrew words are rendered "censer": (1) *maḥtāh,* describing the vessel used for carrying the charcoal on which the incense was burnt. It was of a size sufficient to contain a quantity of live coals, so as to burn at least two handfuls of incense (Leviticus 16:12). It is also rendered "firepans" (Exodus 27:3; 38:3; Numbers 4:14 (R.V.); 2 Kings 25:15; Jeremiah 52:19 and so forth). The two renderings denote the same vessel. These censers were made of bronze (or brass). Those in Solomon's Temple were of gold (1 Kings 7:50; 2 Kings 25:15). The word is rendered "snuffdishes" in Exodus 25:38; 37:23; Numbers 4:9. These were probably not trays for the snuffers, but utensils of the same shape as the censers, in which to receive and take away the burnt parts of the wicks.

(2) Hebrew *miqtereth* is translated "censer" in the two places where the word is found, 2 Chronicles 26:19 and Ezekiel 8:11. In the former, Uzziah dared to take a censer for burning incense in the Temple and was smitten with leprosy. In the latter, the elders of Israel were guilty of committing abominable profanity in Jerusalem. In Numbers 16:46, Aaron was told to take the censer belonging to his ministry as high priest and make atonement to stay the plague. For the ministry of the high priest on the Day of Atonement see Leviticus 16:12, 13.

CLOUD

1. Clouds in connection with rain. See, for example, 1 Kings 18:44. In Proverbs 16:15 the king's favor is as a "cloud of the latter rain," referring to the light showers in March and April which refresh the ripening barley and wheat, bringing a good crop in May and June. On the contrary, in Isaiah 18:4 the Lord says that when He lifts up the ensign to gather Israel, He will be still Himself and be to the nations like a "cloud of dew in the heat

of harvest." That is by way of judgment, for in the autumn harvest of fruits a mere moisture in the sky is unwelcome, causing withering heat. So the dealings of the Lord will be like feverish symptoms among the nations. In Isaiah 25:5 the prophet says that God will bring down the noise of strangers as the heat by the shadow of a cloud. The reference here is probably to the prostrating wind from the desert covering the sky with hot sand clouds, and thus the fierce foe of Israel shall be brought low.

2. Clouds as symbolic of what is fleeting. Job says that "as the cloud is consumed and vanisheth away" so is the brevity of human life (7:9). He complains that his welfare is passed away as a cloud (30:15). In Isaiah 44:22, God declares that He has "blotted out, as a thick cloud," Israel's transgressions, and, "as a cloud," its sins. As a morning cloud at sunrise melts away just afterwards, so God will deal with the sins of His people. In contrast to this, the supposed goodness of Ephraim and Judah is "as a morning cloud" that goes away early and in Hosea 13:3, they themselves would be "as the morning cloud."

3. Clouds as a covering. Job prays that a cloud may dwell upon the day of his birth (3:5). The Lord tells Job that He made the cloud the garment of the sea, like the swaddling clothes of the newborn world. In contrast to this, the combination of power and righteousness in a king, when his justice is tempered with mercy, is like the blessing of a morning without clouds in springtime (2 Samuel 23:4).

4. Clouds as the emblem of God's presence. The bow in the cloud in Genesis 9:14 was indicative of His mercy amidst judgment. Again, His clouds betokened His protecting and guiding presence with Israel in their jour-

neys (Exodus 13:21). So with the cloud that covered the tent of the congregation, making it impossible for Moses to enter (Exodus 40:34–38). See also in connection with the Temple (1 Kings 8:10). At Sinai the Lord said to Moses, "Lo, I come unto thee in a thick cloud" (Exodus 19:9). By this, the mediator whom God had appointed would receive special credentials. His presence was designed also to make known His holiness to the people in contrast to their unholiness (verse 16). Clouds are spoken of as God's chariot (Psalms 104:3; Isaiah 19:1; Ezekiel 10:4) and as the dust of His feet (Nahum 1:3).

God has absolute control over the clouds; He keeps them suspended (Job 26:8); He numbers them and balances them and has a purpose in their spreadings and motions (Job 36:29; 37:16; 38:37; Psalms 78:23). Compare also Acts 1:9 and Revelation 1:7.

CONGREGATION

The chief word used in the Old Testament 'ēdhāh signifies an appointed meeting between God and man. The people of Israel were regarded collectively as a holy community. Anyone who disregarded God's commandments was to be cut off from the congregation of Israel (Exodus 12:19). God cannot permit unholiness among His people. What is called the tabernacle of the congregation was, as in R.V., the tent of meeting (Hebrew 'ōhel mō'ēdh). The explanation of this is given in Exodus 33:7 where Moses used to take the tent (not the Tabernacle, which had not been made) "and pitched it without the camp, afar off from the camp," and he called it "the Tabernacle [tent] of the meeting." Everyone who sought the Lord would go out to the tent of meeting which was outside the camp. When Moses went out there, all the people rose up and stood every man at his tent door looking after Moses, until he was gone into the tent.

In connection with the Tabernacle, God said that He would meet with Israel to speak with them. It would be sanctified with the glory of His presence (Exodus 29:43).

The word *mō'ēdh* is used to denote the assembly itself in connection with the celebration of a feast. Speaking generally, each Israelite was a member of a house; the family was a collection of houses; the tribe was a collection of families; the congregation a collection of tribes. Their assemblings were called convocations (Leviticus 23). Compare Psalms 74:4 where R.V. has "thine assembly," for KJV "thy congregations." So also in Isaiah 14:13; Lucifer the adversary of God boasted that he would exalt his throne above the stars of God, and would sit upon "the mount of congregation" (*harmō'ēdh*). Here Lucifer, the light-bringer or morning star, symbolizes the fallen monarch of Babylon. Pride was Lucifer's sin and caused his downfall. So the king of Babylon defied God, boasting that he would rule over the north, that is, the utmost limits of the earth. But, like Lucifer, he would be brought down to the pit instead of finding his seat among the congregation. The sides of the pit stand in contrast to the sides of the north.

David declares in Psalms 40:10 that he has not concealed God's lovingkindness and truth from "the great congregation" (*qāhāl rab*), that is, the whole nation of Israel convened to worship God at one of the pilgrimage festivals.

COVENANT

The Hebrew word *berîth* is frequently the object of the verb *kārāth*, "to divide or cut in two"; compare the dividing of the parts of the victim mentioned in Genesis 15:9, 10, 17 where, however, the verb is *bāthar*. God entered into a covenant with Abram giving to him and his seed forever the whole land from Egypt to the Euphrates. From the arrangement of the dividing of the parts of the victims came the expression which literally denoted "to cut a covenant" (similar idioms are found in Greek and Latin).

The word "covenant" in its sense of an agreement on the part of each of two contracting parties cannot apply to a covenant between God and man. His covenant is essentially a matter of grace on His part (compare Galatians 3). Accordingly in Psalms 89:28 God's covenant is explained by the accompanying statement of His mercy. Similarly with God's covenant not to destroy the earth again by water (Genesis 9:15). So with regard to His covenant with David and with the Levites, the priests, His ministers (Jeremiah 33:20–22). There He speaks of His covenant of the day and His covenant of the night.

See Hebrew 9:15–18 where the Gospel covenant is distinguished from the legal covenant. Compare also His covenant in connection with the Lord's Supper (Matthew 26:18). The word "everlasting" or "eternal" is used of God's covenant in various places, for example, Leviticus 24:8; 2 Samuel 23:5. See also Deuteronomy 33:9; Jeremiah 33:21; Malachi 2:4.

In contrast to the covenants made by God are those between men, as between Abimelech and Isaac (Genesis 26:28), where an oath was taken by both parties. See also the covenant between Jacob and Laban (Genesis 31:44). In Exodus 24:7, the book of the covenant has reference to the Law as written on the tables of stone.

D

DAYSMAN

The word "day" has been used in various languages for a time of judgment; see *Expository Dictionary of New Testament Words* under "DAY." (Compare 1 Corinthians 4:3 R.V. margin, "man's day," that is, man's judgment.) Hence the word "daysman,"—to denote one who will act as an arbitrator, to adjudicate between two parties. Such an umpire was accustomed to lay his hands on each party to betoken his ability to decide between them and to show his impartiality. Thus Job says, "neither is there any daysman [*môkhîaḥ*] betwixt us, that might lay his hand upon us both" (Job 9:33). A daysman could have been found on an equal footing with Job, but none on equality with Jehovah, the other party, with whom Job had a contention.

DAYSPRING

The dayspring denoted the time of sunrising, or dawn. In the New Testament the Greek word *anatolē* means the rising (that is, of the sun, Luke 1:78) alluding to the coming of the Messiah. In Job 38:12, it is identified with the morning. God asks Job if he commanded the dayspring "to know his place; That it might take hold of the ends of the earth." The tremendous power of the light is set forth in what is said in the latter part of verse 13, where the dayspring shakes the star Sirius from its place. This word *shaḥar* for "dayspring" frequently signifies "the morning," for example, Genesis 19:15; Nehemiah 4:21; Job 41:18; Psalms 139:9; Isaiah 14:12; 58:8. See the margin of Genesis 32:24; in verse 26 "the day breaketh" is, literally, the "ascending of the morning"; in Joshua 6:15, "the dawning of the day" is, literally, "the rising of the morning"; in Job 3:9, margin, "the eyelids of the morning," as in 41:18. See Isaiah 8:20 R.V.; 47:11, margin. In the title of Psalm 22, "Aijeleth ha-Shahar" means "the hind of the morning." The same word is translated "day" also in Judges 19:25; 1 Samuel 9:26; "early" in Psalms 57:8; 108:2.

DEGREE

The word *ma'alāh*, "degree," means step. In the plural it is rendered "degrees" in regard to the time markings on the dial of Ahaz, a kind of sun clock, 2 Kings 20:9, 10, 11; Isaiah 38:8. From signifying a step or stairs, as in 1 Kings 10:19, 20; 2 Kings 9:13; Nehemiah 3:15; 12:37; Ezekiel 40:6, 22 and so forth, the word came to denote a step in rank, 1 Chronicles 17:17 (in Psalms 62:9, "men of high degree" is, literally, "sons of men" and "men of low degree" is, literally, "sons of Adam"). In Ezekiel 11:5, it is translated "the things that come into [your mind]." In Ezra 7:9 it is rendered "to go up"; in Amos 9:6 "stories" (marginal, "ascensions").

The Songs of Degrees are fifteen in number, four by David, one by Solomon, the rest anonymous. The Hebrew words mean "a song for the ascendings" (*shîr ha-ma 'alôth*). Various meanings have been attached to this. The most probable is that what is indicated is the going up to Jerusalem to the three feasts (Exodus 34:24; 1 Kings 12:27, 28). The oldest is Psalm 122, written by David to provide the northern Israelites with a pilgrim song for their journeys to Zion, whither they had been warned to repair after the ark had been moved there from Shiloh. Most of the others relate to the time after the Babylonian Captivity.

DEVOTED

The word *ḥērem* is used of an offering presented to the Lord, whether a field (Leviticus 27:21) or man or beast (verses 28, 29); Numbers 18:14; so Ezekiel 44:29; see also margin. Certain persons, things, and nations were doomed by God to destruction. Deuteronomy 13:15 (R.V. margin), 17 R.V. (for KJV "cursed"). To God alone belongs the prerogative of taking life, as He alone bestows it. Thus Israel was to destroy the Canaanites and their belongings (with certain reservations). In this respect the R.V. rightly renders the word "devoted" (for KJV "accursed") in Joshua 6:17, 18 (verse 18 reads: "and ye, in any wise keep yourselves from the devoted thing, lest when ye have devoted it, ye take of the devoted thing; so should ye make the camp of Israel accursed [margin, devoted])"; see 7:1, 11, 12, 13, 15; in 1 Samuel 15:21, "devoted things" (for KJV "things which should have been utterly destroyed"). See also R.V. 1 Kings 20:42; 1 Chronicles 2:7; Isaiah 34:5 (margin), and 43:28 (margin); Ezekiel 44:29 (margin). In Zechariah 14:11 it is rendered "utter destruction."

DIADEM

The word *miṣnepheth* is almost always the high priest's turban (KJV "mitre"); but in Ezekiel 21:26, where the KJV rightly has "diadem" the reference is to a crown, not the turban of a priest, but the crown of the wicked prince of Israel, "when iniquity shall have an

end" (verse 25). God will overturn that which is high
"until he come whose right it is [to reign]" (verse 27).
This is an echo, probably, of the promise in Genesis
49:10.

The word *ṣānîph*, from the same root as the preceding,
is used (*a*) in Zechariah 3:5 of the turban of the high
priest, spoken of as a diadem (R.V. margin; the text in KJV
and R.V. has "mitre," that is, turban); (*b*) Job declares in
29:14 that his justice was formerly "a robe and a diadem"
(not a priestly turban). In a coming day Israel, restored to
the Lord, will be "a crown of glory in the hand of the
LORD, and a royal diadem in the hand of thy God"
(Isaiah 62:3). Thus the word has the two meanings (1) a
priestly turban, (2) a royal diadem.

The word *sephîrāh* denoted a diadem, in Isaiah 28:5,
where the Lord promises the godly remnant in Israel
that in a coming day He Himself will be "for a crown of
glory, and for a diadem of beauty" to them.

For DIAL see DEGREE

DIVINATION, DIVINER

This is spoken of in Scripture of the false systems of
ascertaining the divine will. The earliest instance in
which the word so rendered is found in the case of
Balaam to whom Balak made application, sending the
elders of Midian with "the rewards of divination in their
hand" (Numbers 22:7). Balaam was evidently well
known as a skillful practicer of this evil. Being brought
into contact with Israel he sought to combine prophecy,
under God's permissive will, with the art of soothsaying
or divination. This attempt to find out the purposes of
God proved his utter ruin. Whatever method he used

was turned to a foul attempt to destroy Israel by immorality (Numbers 22–25). He is called "the soothsayer" in Joshua 13:22 (margin, "diviner").

The practice of divination is associated in Deuteronomy 18:10, 11 with that of augury, of "an enchanter, or a witch, or a charmer, or a consulter with familiar spirits, or a wizard, or a necromancer," all of which have this in common, that under the influence of evil spirits they are deceived into seeking to the spirits of the dead or are actually allured into consultation with the powers of darkness: "For all that do these things are an abomination unto the LORD," and because of them the Lord decreed the expulsion and destruction of the Canaanites.

The evil is put on the same level as rebellion against God (1 Samuel 15:23) and Saul, pursuing this path of resistance against God, ended his career by consulting with a woman who had a familiar spirit, requesting her that she should "divine" for him by this means (1 Samuel 28:7, 8); see also 1 Chronicles 10:13. This was the sin of which the nation became guilty as a whole, and for which, with other evils God sent them into captivity (2 Kings 17:17). Compare Isaiah 3:2 R.V. "diviner," for KJV "prudent." For the lying character of this form of spiritism see Isaiah 44:25; Jeremiah 14:14; 27:9; 29:8; Ezekiel 13:6, 9, 23; 21:23, 29; 22:28; Micah 3:6; 7:11; Zechariah 10:2.

An illustration of the methods adopted in connection with this cult is recorded in the case of the king of Babylon, in his consultation as to attacking Jerusalem. He stood at the parting of two ways "to use divination: he shook the arrows to and fro, he consulted the teraphim, he looked in the liver." This was overruled by God as a judgment upon His apostate people (Ezekiel 21:18–23

R.V.). The arrows marked with the names of places to be taken were shaken together in a quiver to see which would come out first, or were thrown into the air to see which way they pointed, whether to Jerusalem or to Ammon. The inspection of entrails was designed to see what intimation of success or failure there might be, according to their healthy or unhealthy state; compare Hosea 4:12.

For God's condemnation of every form of this evil see Isaiah 8:19, 20. Satan's aim in spiritism is to substitute the power of evil spirits for the authority of the Word of God. The human beings who act as "mediums" between the consulters and the powers of darkness are said in Scripture to have a "familiar spirit." They put the consulters into communication, not with the dead, but with evil spirits. The "witch" of Endor was the controller of a spirit for this purpose. But God interposed and her clairvoyance was interrupted by the appearance of the real Samuel, which startled her, showing that this was not in accordance with the regular methods of her mediumistic activities (1 Samuel 28).

DRAGON

The word *tan* in Jeremiah 14:6, which has been rendered "jackals" (R.V.), probably denotes the large serpents, boas or pythons. The *tannîm* or *tannînîm* are any great monsters, whether of land or sea; the word is translated "great sea-monsters" in Genesis 21 R.V.; so in KJV Lamentations 4:3 (R.V. jackals). In Deuteronomy 32:33, "the poison of dragons" evidently refers to venomous snakes. In the prophecy foretelling the divine overthrow of Israel's foes in a coming day, the land of Idumea is to become "a habitation of dragons," expressive of complete desolation (Isaiah 34:13; contrast the deliverance in 35:7 and 43:20). So with Hazor in Jeremiah 49:33. In Malachi 1:3, Edom has become a desolation already. In Psalms 74:13 "thou breakest the heads of the dragons [margin, "whales"] in the waters" is a reference to Pharaoh and the princes of Egypt (just as crocodiles are the monsters of the Nile). Egypt is similarly referred to in Isaiah 51:9, 10 (Pharaoh was "wounded" not drowned); Babylon in Isaiah 13:22; Jeremiah 51:34, 37 and Ezekiel 29:3. In Isaiah 27:1 "the dragon [R.V. leviathan] that is in the sea" is a description of the pagan power which the Lord will slay in the day of the deliverance of Israel.

On account of the sins of Judah, Jerusalem was to become "a den of dragons" (Jeremiah 9:11; 10:22); see the description of their sins in 14:6, 7. Compare Psalms 44:19.

The serpent is figuratively spoken of as "the dragon" in Psalms 91:13. He who dwells "in the secret place of the Most High," enjoying communion with God (verse 1) will overcome every foe, whether the roaring lion, or the bite of the adder, or the hissing breath of the dragon, each suggestive of spiritual foes and temptations.

Concerning the dragon well in Jerusalem, in Nehemiah 2:13, Jewish tradition ascribes to Solomon the construction of an aqueduct or conduit from "the Pools of Solomon" to supply water for the Temple services; it is supposed to have been called *Tannin* (dragon) from its serpentine course, and the dragon well was an outflow from it in the valley of Hinnom. Others suggest that the serpent was regarded as a sort of guardian, giving healing virtue to the water. The former is certainly the more likely explanation.

E

EBENEZER

This place name, which means "stone of help," is mentioned three times in 1 Samuel. It was the scene of the defeat of Israel by the Philistines, 4:1 and 5:1. In 7:12, when Israel defeated the Philistines, Samuel took a stone and set it between Mizpah (the watchtower) and Shen (the tooth or crag). This may have given the name to the locality mentioned in the earlier chapters.

EMBROIDER, EMBROIDERER (BROIDERED)

(1) The verb *shābaṣ* and the corresponding noun *tashbēṣ* are used of the high priest's coat, Exodus 28:39 (first part), "embroider" (R.V. "weave"); in Exodus 28:4, KJV "a broidered coat" (R.V. "a coat of chequer work"). The coat of the high priest would either be sewn by hand or woven in lines and squares to give the appearance of chequer work and lustre. Compare Exodus 26:1, 31, and so forth.

(2) The noun *riqmāh* and the verb *rāqam* denote needlework. The screen (KJV "hanging") for the door of the Tabernacle was to be made "of blue and purple and scarlet stuff, and fine twined linen, the work of the embroiderer" (Exodus 26:36 R.V.; 27:16; 36:37; 38:18). In Exodus 28:39 (last part) and 39:29, it is used of the girdle, "the work of the embroiderer" (R.V. for KJV "of needlework"). In 35:35 and 38:23, Bezalel and Oholiab (R.V.), men skilled as engravers and embroider-

61

ers, were appointed to such work for the Tabernacle.

In Psalms 139:15, the word is used metaphorically of the bodily frame of the psalmist, as being "curiously wrought" (literally, "embroidered").

In Judges 5:30, Deborah in her song makes the mother of Sisera imagine that he had gained a spoil of many things, among them "a spoil of divers colours of embroidery" (R.V. for KJV "needlework"). In 1 Chronicles 29:2, it is used of stones of "divers colours"; in Ezekiel 17:3, of feathers (margin, "embroidering"). In Psalms 45:14 R.V. has "broidered work," for KJV "raiment of needlework." In Ezekiel 16:10, 13; 27:7, 16, 24, both have "broidered work"; in 16:18 and 26:16 "broidered" garments.

Where the process was that of needlework, the cloth was streched out and fastened in a frame, and sewn work in colored thread was added; or it might be introduced during the weaving. The work of those who were skilled in the occupation is called "cunning work" or "the work of the designer."

For ENCHANTMENT see DIVINATION

EPHOD

(1) The ephod was a priestly garment of white linen, and attached to the body by a girdle. The ephod of the high priest was of a special character. It was oblong in shape and made of richly variegated material, interwoven with gold thread, all the "work of the designer" (see EMBROIDERY). It was kept in place by two shoulder pieces, that is, straps attached to it behind, and passing to the front over the shoulders; on the top of each of these was an onyx stone, engraven with the names of six

of the tribes. It was held round the body by a band of the
same material as the ephod, and woven in one piece
with it by which it was girded round the waist. It was
worn over a blue garment called "the robe of the
ephod." On the front of it was fastened the jewelled
breastplate (Exodus 28:6–8, 15, 27; 29:5; 39:2–5, 19 and
so forth; Leviticus 8:7, 8).

A simpler ephod was worn by Samuel as a servant in
Eli's ministry (1 Samuel 2:18), by the eighty-five priests
slain by Doeg (22:18), and by David when he danced
before the ark (2 Samuel 6:14).

(2) A different kind of ephod was especially connected
with idolatry. Gideon made an ephod of the gold rings
taken from the Midianites and Ishmaelites (Judges 8:27).

F

FACE

This is the KJV rendering of the Hebrew words (1) *'aph* (which has several meanings) which in some passages R.V. gives more exact renderings, such as "nose" (Genesis 24:47); "nostrils" (Ezekiel 38:18); (2) *'ayin*, an eye (for example, "the face of the earth," literally, "the eye," Exodus 10:5, 15; Numbers 22:5; in some passages the R.V. rightly renders by "eyes," for the KJV "face," for example, 1 Kings 20:38, 41; 2 Kings 9:30; Jeremiah 4:30); (3) *pānîm*, connected with *pānāh*, to turn, primarily to turn the face, as in Isaiah 45:22, "Look [literally, "turn"] unto me." The noun *pānîm* is used, however, in a great variety of applications, both literally and metaphorically. The face or countenance was frequently used to signify the "presence" of a person (the face being the noblest part), for example, Deuteronomy 25:9; 2 Samuel 24:4; it is constantly said of God, for example, Genesis 3:8; Exodus 33:14, 15. Hence, from the implied permission or invitation to approach, it came to denote favor or acceptance, spoken of as "the light of the countenance" (for example, Psalms 89:15); on the contrary to withhold the face or turn it away indicated disapproval or rejection (for example, Psalms 13:1; 27:9; 88:14; 143:7).

The noun is often used in connection with paying regard to persons, for example, Deuteronomy 10:17; 28:50; 2 Kings 3:14; in the following places a different verb is used, signifying to recognize the presence of a person (that is, unjustly), Deuteronomy 1:17; 16:19; Proverbs 24:23; 28:21.

The shewbread was literally called "the bread of the face," that is, presence bread, Exodus 25:30; 35:13; 1 Samuel 21:6; 1 Kings 7:48. It was placed in two rows of six cakes each on the table of acacia wood in the Holy Place of the Tabernacle, with frankincense. The word rendered "shewbread" thus betokened the representation of the tribes of Israel before God continually. The cakes typify Christ as God's provision for all His people. The fine flour typified the sinless humanity of Christ.

When used with the personal pronoun, for example, "my face," it was sometimes a circumlocution for the person himself, that is, me, thee, and so forth. Hence the R.V. has "them" for "their face" in Exodus 14:19, and "thee" for "thy face" in Genesis 30:33; Deuteronomy 9:3; 28:7; in Jeremiah 17:16 the KJV has "thee" and the R.V. "thy face."

To spit in the face was the utmost possible sign of scorn and hatred (Numbers 12:14; Deuteronomy 25:9; Job 30:10; Isaiah 50:6; see also Matthew 26:67; 27:30).

To have the face covered by another person was a sign of doom (Esther 7:8). For a person to cover his own face was a token of modesty, self-abasement, humility or worship, as with the veils of women (Genesis 24:65); so in the case of Elijah and his mantle (1 Kings 19:13). The seraphim cover their faces with their wings (Isaiah 6:2).

For FAMILIAR SPIRIT see DIVINATION

FAT

The fat "that was upon the inwards" of a sacrificial animal was set apart to God as being the richest part. All the fat was the Lord's (Leviticus 3:14–16). The fat of the kidneys was indicative of the excellence and vigor of the animal.

In the animal the fat was likewise the source of its nutriment, and in this respect, it was especially appropriate as an offering to Jehovah. In the peace offerings, "an offering made by fire," the fat tail was to be taken away entire "hard by the backbone" (Leviticus 3:9), that is, where the pad of fat begins.

The expression "the fat" of anything accordingly signifies the choicest part, as in such phrases as "the fat of the land" (Genesis 45:18), "all the fat of the oil and all the fat of the vintage, and of the corn" (Numbers 18:12, margin), "the fat of kidneys of wheat" (Deuteronomy 32:14), "the fat of the mighty" (2 Samuel 1:22). Compare Psalms 78:31; Isaiah 10:16.

FILLET

This is the translation of two words: (1) *hût*, which denotes a thread. In the KJV of Jeremiah 52:21, it is used of that which compassed the pillars made by Solomon for the Temple (margin, "thread"; R.V. "line"; both KJV and R.V. translate it "line" in 1 Kings 7:15; compare Joshua 2:18); (2) *hāshûq*, always in the plural, "fillets," the connecting rods which joined the pillars together in the Tabernacle; those of the pillars of the court were overlaid with silver (typical of redemption), those of the pillars of the screen at the door with gold (Exodus 27:10, 11; 36:38; 38:10–12, 17, 19); entrance is based upon the righteousness and glory of God.

The corresponding verb *hishshaq*, to furnish with fillets, is translated "filleted" in Exodus 27:17; 38:17, 28 (R.V. "made fillets for them").

FIRMAMENT

While this English word is derived from the Latin *firmamentum* which signifies firmness or strengthening (like the Greek *stereōma*), the Hebrew word, *rāqîaʻ*, has no such meaning, but denoted the "expanse," that which is stretched out. Certainly the sky was not regarded as a hard vault in which the heavenly orbs were fixed. What is called the "firmament" in Genesis 1 from verses 6–20; Psalms 19:1; 150:1; Ezekiel 1:22–26; 10:1; and Daniel 12:3, finds an explanatory description in Psalms 104:2, "who stretchest out the heavens like a curtain," and similarly in Isaiah 40:22, with the addition, "and spreadeth them out as a tent to dwell in."

The whole expanse includes the atmosphere encircling the earth, the locality of the clouds (Genesis 1:6, 7, 20), and the region in which are the sun, moon and stars (verse 14). Language connected with it is often metaphorical and phenomenal; see, for example, Genesis 7:11, "windows of heaven" (compare Isaiah 24:18); Psalms 78:23, "the doors of heaven." The figurative language in Job 37:18, "Hast thou with him spread out the sky, which is strong, and as a molten looking glass?" does not convey the idea of solidity, but that of clearness, transparency and brightness; compare Exodus 24:10, "the body of heaven [that is, the very heaven itself] in [its] clearness." The transparent character of the firmament is indicated in that part of Ezekiel's vision recorded in 1:26.

There is therefore nothing in the language of the original to suggest that the writers were influenced by the imaginative ideas of heathen nations.

FIRSTBORN

Special privileges attached to primogeniture in patriarchal times, as in the case of Esau and Jacob (Genesis
25:23–33), and Reuben (49:3; 1 Chronicles 5:1). A special birthright and a larger portion of the inheritance
were given to the firstborn; see also Exodus 22:29. But
the right was not merely a matter of birth; it might be
sold; a biased father might bestow it on a younger son,
though such a thing was forbidden by God (Deuteronomy 21:15–17).

In the nation of Israel the eldest son in the family was
regarded as sacred to God, because all the Israelite
firstborn were exempted from the divine judgment executed upon the Egyptians when their firstborn were destroyed on the night of the Passover.

The tribe of Levi was substituted for all the firstborn in
Israel to minister to the Lord (Numbers 3:12, 45, 50). As
there were 273 more firstborn in Israel than the males in
Levi, the 273 were redeemed at five shekels each. But in
order to mark the consecration of the whole nation to
Jehovah, the redemption money was exacted for every
firstborn (Numbers 18:15). The firstlings of cattle were to
be offered to the Lord. An ass was either to be redeemed
with a lamb or slain (Exodus 13:13), for the ass's colt was
unfit for sacrifice.

(For the subject of Christ as the Firstborn, see *Expository Dictionary of New Testament Words* under
"FIRST-BEGOTTEN, FIRSTBORN.")

FIRSTFRUITS

Just as the whole nation of Israel was consecrated to
God by the consecration of the firstborn, so the produce
of the land was set apart to God by the consecration of

the firstfruits (see Exodus 22:29; Leviticus 23:10 and Numbers 15:18–21 and compare Romans 11:16). The firstfruits of the oil, wine, and wheat were to be offered for the benefit of the priests as the Lord's reprensentatives (Numbers 18:11–13).

In connection with the three annual feasts, (1) at the Passover, "on the morrow after the sabbath," a sheaf of fresh corn (barley) of the firstfruits of the crop was to be waved "before the LORD" (Leviticus 23:10–14). (2) At Pentecost "two wave loaves of two tenth deals . . . of fine flour" (that is, wheaten flour, the wheat coming later than the barley) were to be "baken with leaven; they are the firstfruits unto the LORD." With these were to be presented "seven lambs without blemish of the first year, and one young bullock, and two rams," all as a burnt offering, "with their meal offering, and their drink offerings, even an offering made by fire, of a sweet savour unto the LORD." Besides all this, "one kid of the goats for a sin offering, and two lambs of the first year for a sacrifice of peace offerings." The whole of these offerings were to be waved "with the bread of the firstfruits for a wave offering before the LORD, with the two lambs," all being "holy to the LORD for the priest" (Leviticus 23:16–20). (3) The Feast of Tabernacles, on the fifteenth day of the seventh month was itself a definite acknowledgment of the firstfruits of the harvest; for that feast was to be kept when the fruits of the land had been gathered in (verse 39).

Beside these offerings at the feasts there were to be individual offerings, and it is significant that in Exodus 22:29, the two are combined, namely, the immediate offering of the firstfruits ("the abundance"—R.V. margin "thy fulness and thy tear"), "and of the liquors," and the presentation of "the firstborn of thy sons." Also there was to be a heave offering of the first dough baked (Numbers 15:19, 21).

The individual offered his firstfruits in a basket at the Tabernacle or Temple, acknowledging to the Lord that he had come to the promised country. After the priest had placed the basket before the altar, the offerer acknowledged that his father (Jacob) was a wandering Aramean who went down to Egypt (Deuteronomy 26:1–11).

The offerings were either raw produce (*bikkûrîm*) or prepared produce (*terûmôth*). Fruit trees were to be looked upon as uncircumcised (that is, profane) for three years. The produce of the fourth year was devoted to God. Only in the fifth year did the fruit become the owner's (Leviticus 19:23–25). See Ezekiel 20:40; 44:30; 48:14; Malachi 3:8.

After periods of the neglect of these duties there were two reformations, one under Hezekiah (2 Chronicles 31:5, 11), the other under Nehemiah (Nehemiah 10:35, 37; 12:44).

The lesson of these injunctions for believers today is that they may present themselves and all that they have to the Lord.

For FOUNTAIN see WELL

FRANKINCENSE

The Hebrew word is *lebônāh* from *lāban*, to be white, and denotes a glittering vegetable resin, used for burning at sacrifices (Exodus 30:7, 8, 34–36). It was imported from Arabia (Isaiah 60:6; Jeremiah 6:20), and was obtained by incision in the bark of the tree. It was mingled with other perfumes, as in Song of Solomon 3:6, in the description of Solomon's litter.

Frankincense symbolizes prayer accepted with God (Psalms 141:2; see also Malachi 1:11 and Revelation 5:8 R.V.; 8:3, 4). The time of the offering of incense, morning and evening, was the time of prayer (Luke 1:10).

For FRONTLETS see "PHYLACTERIES" in *Expository Dictionary of New Testament Words*

FULLER

The Hebrew word *kōbēs* is from *kābas*, to tread. Fulling, or cleansing, cloth was carried out by stamping on the garments with the feet (or with bats) in tubs of water containing some alkaline dissolved, such as soap, or niter, a potash which mixed with oil was used as soap (Proverbs 25:20; Jeremiah 2:22; Malachi 3:2). The niter is not saltpeter but native carbonate of soda. Chalk or some sort of earth was used to whiten garments. The trade was carried outside Jerusalem to avoid offensive smells. The fuller's field mentioned in Isaiah 7:3 and 36:2 contained a raised causeway in which was the conduit of the upper pool, an important part of Jerusalem's water supply. There God encouraged Ahaz through Isaiah (Isaiah 7:3). Thither Rabshakeh advanced to a convenient place near the temple walls, to utter his boastful threat (10:28, 32, with 36:2).

The white garment is symbolic of the righteousness of Christ and of His people. Hence the exhortation "Let thy garments be always white" (Ecclesiastes 9:8; compare Revelation 3:4, 5, 18; 19:8). Compare also the transfiguration garments of Christ, "exceeding white as snow; so as no fuller on earth can whiten them" (Mark 9:3).

G

For GALL see *Expository Dictionary of New Testament Words*

GALLERY

In Song of Solomon 1:17 the KJV and R.V. rightly have "rafters" (for the KJV margin "galleries"), the reference being to the crossbeams on the fretted work of the carved ceiling Hebrew *rāḥîṭîm*. In 7:5, for Hebrew *rahaṭ*, the R.V. accurately has "tresses" (for the KJV "galleries"). The word is found elsewhere only in Genesis 30:38 and Exodus 2:16, where it has the meaning "watering troughs" or "gutters."

A different word (Hebrew *'attûq*) is used in Ezekiel 41:15 and 42:3, where the "galleries" are terrace buildings or perhaps colonnades. Some suggest a word meaning walls. An explanation (identifying the galleries with the pillars) of why the upper chambers are shorter, ascribes this to the absence of supporting pillars, which allowed an extra length to the lower story chambers. Thus the space included within the pillars would form an open gallery.

For GIANTS see ANAKIM

GIRDLE

1. The *'abnēṭ* was the priest's girdle, made of gold, blue, purple, scarlet and fine-twined linen (Exodus 28:4, 39, 40; 39:29). This girdle for the coat was to be "the work of the embroiderer," the skilled weaver. The high

priest's girdle on the day of atonement was of white linen only (Leviticus 16:4).

2. The 'ēzôr was a girdle worn by men only (2 Kings 1:8; Job 12:18). There was a common girdle, made of leather, and a finer girdle, made of linen (Jeremiah 13:1, 2, 4, 6, 7, 10, 11). This word is used metaphorically of righteousness and faithfulness (Isaiah 11:5, twice). The ḥagôr was a belt fastened by a clasp or tied in a knot, the ends hanging in front. Such a girdle was costly. Jonathan made a present of his to David, 1 Samuel 18:4 (see also 2 Samuel 18:11; 20:8; 1 Kings 2:5).

To gird up the loins signified to be ready for action (see Luke 12:35; Ephesians 6:14; 1 Peter 1:13).

Note: The ḥesheb, described as the "curious girdle" of the ephod, in the KJV of Exodus 28:8, 27, 28; 29:5; 39:5 was simply, as in R.V. a "cunningly woven band," attached to the ephod.

GLORY

The Hebrew word kābōdh, denoting glory, honor (the most frequent word), literally means "weight," hence Paul's mention of the "eternal weight of glory" (2 Corinthians 4:17). The phrase "my glory" has reference to the tongue, in Psalms 16:9 (compare Acts 2:26); 30:12 (margin); 57:8; 108:1. The tongue, as the interpreter of the soul, is the glory of man as superior to the brute; it is that by which he glorifies God, and therefore as associated with the soul, is man's highest glory.

The Hebrew word hādār signifies that which is beauteous, excellent, majestic. It is rendered "glory" in Deuteronomy 33:17 (KJV; "majesty" in R.V.); Psalms 90:16; Isaiah 2:10, 19:21; 5:14; Micah 2:9. The associated word heder is rendered "glory" in Daniel 11:20. The word ṭōhar signifying purity or brightness is rendered "glory" in the KJV of Psalms 89:44 (R.V. "brightness"). The Aramaic word *yeqār*, however, is rendered "glory" in Daniel 2:37; 4:36; 5:18; 7:14. Hebrew *sebhî* denoting that which is prominent, conspicuous (like a roe, another meaning of the word) is rendered "glory" in Isaiah 13:19; 23:9; 24:16; 28:5; Ezekiel 20:6, 15; 25:9; 26:20. Hebrew *'addereth*, signifying something ample, is rendered "glory," in Zechariah 11:3. Hebrew *hôdh*, "grandeur" (that is, an imposing form and appearance) is rendered "glory" in Job 39:20; 40:10; Psalms 45:3; 148:13; Jeremiah 22:18; Habakkuk 3:3; Zechariah 6:13. Hebrew *tiph'ereth*, an ornament, is rendered "glory" in several places, for example, 1 Chronicles 22:5; 29:11; Psalms 78:61; 89:17; Proverbs 4:9; 16:31; 17:6; 19:11; 20:29; 28:12; Isaiah 10:12; 20:5; 46:13; 60:7, and so forth.

A man's glory sometimes signifies his material prosperity (for example, Isaiah 61:6). So in regard to the glory of nations (Haggai 2:7) the glory of the king or a nation consists in the warriors that indicate his or its might (Isaiah 8:7; 17:3; 21:16). Glory may stand for reputation, as in 2 Samuel 6:20; Job 29:20; Psalms 4:2.

The glory of Jehovah signifies His Self-revealed Being and character (for example, Exodus 33:17–23; Isaiah 6:3, margin). Sometimes the glory of Jehovah denotes a physical phenomenon and indicates His presence (for example, Ezekiel 1:28; 11:23).

God is the glory of His saints (Jeremiah 2:11), and they are His glory (Isaiah 62:3; Jeremiah 13:11).

For GO'EL see KINSMAN

GROVE

Two words are translated "grove" in KJV, and both are ancient mistranslations. (1) Asherah was a Canaanite and

Phoenician goddess (Exodus 34:13 R.V. margin, the consort of the supreme god). The word *'ashērāh* also signified the image of the goddess. Maachah, the mother of Asa, made "an abominable image for an Asherah" (1 Kings 15:13 R.V. [or rather "for Asherah," the goddess, as in the margin]). Manasseh set an image in the Temple (2 Kings 21:7). Prophets were associated with the worship (1 Kings 18:19 R.V. "prophets of the Asherah"). Women wove hangings for the goddess (2 Kings 23:7). The plural "the Asheroth" (that is, "the images") is mentioned in Judges 3:7, in connection with the worship of the Baalim (the plural of Baal). The more common plural is *Asherim* as in Exodus 34:13. The worship was also associated with that of Astarte, the deity of the planet Venus, the principal goddess of the Sidonians (1 Kings 11:5, "Ashtoreth"). All this kind of worship was prohibited by God (Exodus 34:13). It was accompanied by the most licentious rites. It was carried on under the shade of trees and on high hills (Deuteronomy 12:2; 1 Kings 14:23). Images of the goddess were made of wood (1 Kings 15:13); or an Asherah could be a tree planted or fixed (Deuteronomy 16:21).

The worship of sacred trees may have sprung from a corrupted distortion of what had been handed down in connection with the tree of life and the tree of knowledge (Genesis 3). Such corruption would lead naturally to the abominable practices associated with all such worship (see Romans 1:22–28).

(2) The word *'ēshel*, translated "grove" in Genesis 21:33, denotes a "tamarisk tree" (R.V.). Abraham planted it in Beersheba as a testimony to his recognition of God's dealings with him (see the same word in 1 Samuel 22:6 and 31:13 R.V.).

H

HABERGEON

This denotes a coat of mail, covering the neck and chest. The high priest's robe of the ephod was to have "a hole for the head in the midst thereof" and "a binding of woven work round about the hole of it, as it were the hole of a coat of mail" (Exodus 28:31, 32; R.V. for KJV "habergeon"), the object being to prevent its being rent.

HANGING, HANGINGS

The word *māsākh* is used to signify (1) the curtain closing the entrance to the Tabernacle from the court outside (Exodus 26:36, 37, R.V. "screen"; so 35:15; 39:38; 40:5 and so forth); (2) the hanging which closed the entrance to the court itself (Exodus 35:17; 38:18 and so forth, R.V. "screening"); (3) the veil screening off the Holy of Holies from the rest of the Tabernacle (Numbers 3:31, R.V. "screen"); compare Exodus 35:12; 39:34; 40:21, R.V.

The word *qelā'îm* denotes the hangings of fine-twined linen for the walls of the court of the Tabernacle. These were suspended from pillars and shut off the court from the outer world (Exodus 27:9, 11 and so forth). They are more fully described as "the hangings of the court" (Exodus 35:17; 38:9 and so forth).

Where it is said in 2 Kings 23:7, that "women wove hangings for the grove [Asherah]," the margin (KJV and R.V.) states that the Hebrew word signifies "houses," but the R.V. margin translates it "tents" (that is, for the image of the goddess).

For HELL see SHEOL

HIGH PLACES

These were chosen as local sanctuaries for the purposes of worship, especially that of an idolatrous character (for example, Leviticus 26:30; Numbers 21:28; 33:52; Isaiah 15:2; 16:12). The high places thus became polluted; sacrifices and incense were offered on them, with the licentious rites associated with them (2 Kings 12:3; 14:4; 15:35; 23:9). They were condemned by God-fearing kings, but there was a certain amount of toleration by others, when the places were devoted to the worship of Jehovah (2 Chronicles 33:17).

By the time of Jeroboam, the high places of Dan and Bethel had been in constant use even by Israelites in these parts who professed to acknowledge God. It became easy therefore for him to persuade the people to forgo the journey to Jerusalem in order to fulfill the divine commands. He made in Bethel and Dan "houses of high places" (1 Kings 12:31 R.V.) and made "priests from among all the people, which were not of the sons of Levi."

Eventually the term *bāmôth,* "high places," became commonly used in a general way, and came to signify a shrine in a city or in a valley (see 2 Kings 17:9; Jeremiah 7:31; Ezekiel 16:31). In Ezekiel 16:16 Israel is reproached for setting up tents hung with colored tapestry for their idolatry, after the manner of harlots (compare 2 Kings 23:7, R.V. "for Asherah").

In Ezekiel 20:29 God asks the idolatrous house of Israel, "What meaneth the high place whereunto ye go [or come]?" Then follows the statement, "So the name thereof is called Bamah [that is, "high place"] unto this day." The significance lies in this, that the two parts of the name (Ba-mah) form part of the question in the original, "What [mah] is the Bamah whereunto ye come [bā']?" Divine and withering scorn is thus poured upon these apostates. They ought to have abandoned the place with its name. All that they did there was an abomination and a provocation to God (verse 28), and would inevitably bring His judgments upon them (verses 33–38).

There is an apparent discrepancy in the records concerning the high places in the reign of Asa: 1 Kings 15:14 states that they were not taken away; 2 Chronicles 14:3 states that Asa took them away (so verse 5), whereas 15:17 says they were not taken away. It seems probable that at first a definite measure was taken to do away with them, but that later on the general usage on the part of the people, especially where a profession was made of devoting the worship to the God of Israel, led to a retention for such purposes; where they were renewed or retained for idolatry, a godly king like Asa put them away entirely.

The practice was so deep rooted that the removal was made a taunt by Rabshakeh against Hezekiah, as if such an act was forsooth derogatory to Jehovah's honor. He was aware that the removal had roused the enmity of many of the Jews (2 Kings 18:22).

HORN

The usual word for "horn" is qeren. The horn was used as a trumpet, which at first seems to have been a horn perforated at the tip. In Joshua 6:5, it is mentioned as the horn of a ram. In verses 4, 5, 6, 8, 13 another word, *yōbēl*, is used, translated "ram's horn," or the plural; this word is connected with *yābal*, to flow or stream forth, and the rendering might better be "jubilee trumpets." These verses and Exodus 19:13 are the only places where the word is used of a trumpet (see JUBILEE).

The horn (*qeren*) was used as a flask to contain oil (for example, 1 Samuel 16:1), or some other material like antimony for beautifying the eyelashes or eyelids of women; hence the name given to one of Job's daughters, Keren-happuch, "horn of [beauty] stibium" (Job 42:14), in contrast to Job 16:15.

The horn, as the instrument of the strength of an animal, is used as the emblem of power. It is said to be "exalted" when the significance is the show of power (Psalms 89:17, 24; 92:10; 112:9; 148:14); when it is said to be cut off or broken, it is symbolic of destruction (Jeremiah 48:25). It is used in the same metaphorical way with the meaning of arrogance (Psalms 75:4, 5, "Lift not up the horn . . . speak not with a stiff neck"). In Isaiah 5:1 it is used of a fruitful hill, where there was a vineyard, "a vineyard in the horn of the son of oil" (see KJV margin). In Habakkuk 3:4 KJV, "he had horns coming out of his hand" would be suggestive of power; so with R.V. "rays coming forth from his hand" (KJV margin, "bright beams"), which might signify lightning flashes; the corresponding verb, *qāran*, to horn, is used of Moses' face emitting rays (Exodus 34:29, 30, 35, the skin of his face "shone"); hence the symbolic horns, for example, on the head of Michelangelo's Moses.

"The horns of the altar" (Exodus 27:2; 29:12; Leviticus 4:7) were four projections, to which the sacrificial victim was bound (Psalms 118:27). They were smeared with blood in consecrating priests (Exodus 29:12) and in the sin offering (Leviticus 4:7). To grasp them was symbolic of laying hold of the strength of Jehovah, so as to have a place of refuge (1 Kings 1:50, 51).

The horn is also used symbolically of world powers. The four horns of Zechariah 1:18 are four Gentile powers which have oppressed and scattered the Jewish people. The ten horns of Daniel 7:7 and the four horns of Daniel 8:8 are successors of Alexander the Great, who is himself signified by the "notable horn" of the he-goat in Daniel 8:5. The ram with two horns in Daniel 8:3 represents the dual Medo-Persian monarchy. The "little horn" of Daniel 7:8 and 8:9 is Antiochus Epiphanes (175–164 B.C.), the historical prototype of the Antichrist, portrayed as the beast from the sea in Revelation 13:1.

I

IMAGE, IMAGERY

The word "image" in the Old Testament translates a number of Hebrew words with different meanings. They are as follows:

(1) *ṣelem*, a copy or counterpart, for example, Genesis 1:26, 27; 5:3; 9:6; Numbers 33:52; 1 Samuel 6:5, 11; 2 Kings 11:18; Amos 5:26. In Psalms 39:6 this word is translated "vain shew" (R.V. "shadow"—not a good rendering).

(2) *sēmel*, a resemblance or likeness, Ezekiel 8:3, 5. This word is rendered "figure" in Deuteronomy 4:16 and "idol" in 2 Chronicles 33:7, 15.

(3) *temûnāh*, a similitude, Job 4:16; elsewhere "likeness," Exodus 20:4, or "similitude," Numbers 12:8; Deuteronomy 4:12, 15, 16. The R.V. has "form" everywhere but "likeness" in Psalms 17:15.

(4) *maskîth*, a picture or representation, "image" in Leviticus 26:1 (R.V. "figured"). In Psalms 73:7, where the KJV has "they have more than heart could wish" (see margin) the R.V. has "the imaginations." Compare Proverbs 18:11; in Proverbs 25:11 "pictures," R.V. "baskets"; but see R.V. margin. It is rendered "imagery" in Ezekiel 8:12.

(5) *maṣṣēbāh*, a pillar and usually so rendered but "image" or "standing image" in KJV, Leviticus 26:1, margin, "pillar"; so in Micah 5:13.

(6) *hammānîm*, actually Canaanite incense altars,

rendered "images" in Leviticus 26:30; 2 Chronicles 14:5; 34:4 (but "idols" in 34:7); Isaiah 17:8; 27:9; Ezekiel 6:4, 6 (R.V. "sun-images").

(7) *terāphîm*, household gods, a word always transliterated in the R.V. and in the KJV in Judges 17:5; 18:14, 17, 18, 20; Hosea 3:4; "images" in Genesis 31:19 and so forth, with the singular "image" in 1 Samuel 19:13, 16.

(8) *'aṣabbîm*, almost always translated "idols" but "images" in 2 Samuel 5:21; in Jeremiah 50:2 KJV "images." The word is a contemptuous term.

(9) *gillûlîm*, properly idol blocks, a term of disparagement, used many times in Ezekiel and nine times elsewhere. It is translated "idols" everywhere except in Jermiah 50:2 KJV "images." Both words in that verse are terms of contempt.

(10) *'elîl*, "worthlessness," a word often applied derisively to foreign gods. In Jeremiah 14:14, "a thing of nought"; in Zechariah 11:17, R.V. "worthless"; in Job 13:4, "of no value."

(11) *pesel*, from a verb meaning to carve, always translated "graven image" in both KJV and R.V. but "carved image" in the KJV of Judges 18:18; 2 Chronicles 33:7. The plural, *pesîlîm*, always translated "graven images" except Judges 3:19, 26 where both versions have "quarries" but "graven images" rightly in the margin. KJV has "carved images" in 2 Chronicles 33:22; 34:3, 4.

(12) *massēkhāh*, literally "a pouring out" is used of molten metal; a "molten calf" in Exodus 32:4, 8 and so forth; "molten image" in Deuteronomy 9:12 and so forth. In Exodus 34:17 and Leviticus 19:4 it is simply rendered "molten" with a separate word for "gods." In Isaiah 30:1 it is rendered "covering." From the same root is the word *nesekh*, a drink offering and usually so rendered

but "molten image" in Isaiah 41:29; 48:5; Jeremiah
10:14; 51:17.

(For the New Testament use of the word see *Expository Dictionary of New Testament Words* under
"IMAGE.")

J

JEALOUS, JEALOUSY

In certain passages God says, "I am a jealous God (*'ēl qannā'*)" (Exodus 20:5; 34:14; Deuteronomy 4:24; 5:9; Joshua 24:19; Nahum 1:2). While the word is used in our language in an evil sense, it has a somewhat different meaning, especially in the Old Testament. It is often used in connection with the marriage relation, and, in this respect, the relation between Jehovah and Israel. Just as jealousy in husband or wife is the forceful assertion of an exclusive right, so God asserts His claim, and vindicates it, on those who are His sole possession. As to His spiritual relation to Israel, see, for example, Isaiah 54:5; 62:5; Hosea 2:19. He thus claims that He is to Israel as husband is to wife, and accordingly idolatry and wickedness in every form are spiritual adultery. His people in their evil ways are represented as provoking Him to jealousy (Deuteronomy 32:16, 21; 1 Kings 14:22; Psalms 78:58; Zephaniah 1:18; 3:8; see also Numbers 25:11 and compare 1 Corinthians 10:22); the expression is especially frequent in Ezekiel (see 16:38, 42; 23:25; 36:5, 6; 38:19; 39:25), but is used also in Hosea 2:2, 16; Joel 2:18; Zephaniah 1:18; Zechariah 1:14; 8:2.

The law of the jealousy offering is declared in Numbers 5:11–31. The application to the priest constituted an appeal to God, to whom the appeal was made to decide the question of the guilt or innocence of the suspected person.

The word is used also to denote a man's passionate concern for the honour of God, as in the cases of Phinehas (Numbers 25:11, 13; Psalms 106:30); Elijah (1 Kings 19:10), Jehu (2 Kings 10:16). Compare Psalms 69:9; John 2:17; Romans 10:2; 2 Corinthians 11:2.

JUBILEE OR JUBILE

The word jubilee in the Hebrew is *yōbēl* from *yābal*, to flow, and is rendered "trumpet" in Exodus 19:13 (see HORN). At the end of every forty-nine years, on the Day of Atonement, the trumpet of jubilee was to be sounded. The Lord commanded Israel that "thou shalt number seven sabbaths of years unto thee, seven times seven years; and the space of the seven sabbaths of years shall be unto thee forty and nine years. Then shalt thou cause the trumpet of the jubile to sound on the tenth day of the seventh month, in the day of atonement shall ye make the trumpet sound throughout all your land" (Leviticus 25:8, 9). Every fiftieth year was to be hallowed, and liberty proclaimed to all inhabitants; it was a time for remembering God's mercy and provision and for exercising compassion.

As far as was possible, the year of jubile(e) restored the people to the original standing which they had had fifty years previously. Property was to be recovered by its original owners, and each man returned to his own family and possessions. Debtors were to be released from their debts, slaves from their bonds, and no property could be sold. If a man, through poverty, were forced to sell part of his property, it was the duty of his kinsman to redeem it, or, if there were no kinsman, the original owner might buy it back (Leviticus 25:25–27). The one exception was in the case of houses built in walled towns, thus making a distinction between houses, which were built by man, and the land, which was God's (25:29–31). The celebration of jubilee in the fiftieth year prevented a man from accumulating too much land, while it saved others from destitution; it was a constant reminder that the Lord had brought His people out of slavery to the Promised Land, of which He was the supreme Owner.

The year of jubilee was the culmination of the sabbatical years, which occurred every seventh year, and which were to be observed as "a sabbath of rest unto the land, a sabbath for the LORD" (Leviticus 25:4). After working the land for six years, for one year it had to lie fallow and, as in the year of jubilee, there was to be no planting, pruning, or reaping. God would meet their need in the seventh year by His provision in the sixth (25:20, 21).

K

KINSMAN

This is one of the meanings of the word *gō'ēl* (the others being redeemer and avenger). The kinsman had three rights, (1) to purchase back the forfeited inheritance for an Israelite who, owing to poverty, had sold his land, as Boaz did for Ruth (4:3–5), or to hold land in possession for a poor kinsman till the year of jubilee (see JUBILEE), Leviticus 25:10–28; (2) to ransom his kinsman from bondage to a foreigner (Leviticus 25:47–49); (3) to avenge the death of his slain kinsman, as a point of honor. Job combines all three in his assurance of faith as to his *Gō'el* (Job 19:25–27, where "upon the earth" should be "over my dust"); this is sufficient to show that he was not suffering because of his guilt. In all three respects Christ is His people's *gō'ēl:* by incarnation, saving them from eternal disinheritance (Hebrews 2:14–18), by redemption (1 Peter 1:18f.; compare Isaiah 49:26), and by avenging them in overcoming by His own death the one who had the power of death (Hebrews 2:14f.).

KNOP

This is an English variant of the word knob. Two distinct Hebrew words are rendered "knop": (1) *kaphtōr.* This denotes a spherical ornament on the stem and the branches or arms of the golden lampstand in the Tabernacle. They were made "of one piece" with the

lampstand itself. For the description see Exodus 25:31–
36 R.V. The cups, the knops, and the flowers were made
with the branches, three of which were on one side of
the stand and three on the other. "Their knops and their
branches shall be of one piece with it: the whole of it one
beaten work of pure gold" (verse 36).

The same word is found in two other passages: in
Amos 9:1, where the KJV renders it "lintel" (margin
"knop"), R.V. "chapiters"; the reference is to the
spherical-shaped capitals of the pillars in the idolatrous
temple at Bethel, where one of the idol calves was set
up. The word implies that which crowns a work at its top
(like the capitals of the pillars in 1 Kings 7:41). In
Zephaniah 2:14, where KJV has "upper lintels," the margin and R.V. have "chapiters," the reference being to the
tops of the columns in ruined Nineveh.

(2) *peqā'îm* a word connected with *paqqû'āh*, a wild
gourd (as in 2 Kings 4:39), though some would suggest a
connection with a word denoting a ball of yarn. This
describes the ornamentation of the cedar lining of the
Temple walls: "and there was cedar on the house
within, carved with knops [margin, "gourds"] and open
flowers" (1 Kings 6:18 R.V.). The reference is probably to
gourdlike oval ornaments, running in straight rows,
carved in the cedarwood wainscot. The word is used also
in chapter 7:24, of the two rows of the same ornamentation under the brim of the molten sea in the Temple
court. These latter knops were not carved but were cast
with the sea.

L

LAMP

More than one Hebrew word is rendered "lamp" in the Old Testament. Hebrew *lappîdh* is used in Genesis 15:17 for the burning lamp (R.V. "flaming torch") which appeared to Abram on the day that the Lord made a covenant with him. The same word is found in Judges 7:16 and 20 for the lamps (R.V. "torches") which Gideon placed "within the pitchers" for the men of Israel, when they prepared to put to flight the Midianites. The "lamp that burneth" typified the salvation of Jerusalem in Isaiah 62:1.

The Hebrew word *nēr* is thought to be more properly a lamp with oil and wick, used, for example, in the description of the golden lampstand of the Tabernacle (see Exodus 25:37); also of the lamps made by Solomon for the Temple (2 Chronicles 4:20).

Lamps were the usual means of illumination. It was probable that they were kept burning all night, as in the case of the virtuous woman whose "candle [R.V. "lamp"] goeth not out by night" (Proverbs 31:18). The "putting out of the light" signified the downfall of the family and the forsaking of their house (compare 2 Samuel 21:17). Lamps appear also to have been kept burning before the teraphim. (See Job 18:6 R.V.; 21:17 R.V.) See CANDLE.

LAMPSTAND

The Hebrew *menôrāh*, rendered "candlestick" in Exodus 25, is properly "lampstand." The simple bowls with a small lip, used by the children of Israel, were gradually developed into lamps with bases. The earlier form was often no more than a shallow saucer, with the rim pinched on one side to form a channel for the wick. At the opposite side there could be a small handle. In the Tabernacle stood an elaborate golden lampstand (verses 31–37). Aramaic *nebrashtā*, rendered "candlestick" in Daniel 5:5, when the fingers of a man's hand appeared and wrote on the wall of King Belshazzar's palace, is used only once in the Old Testament.

For LEAVEN see *Expository Dictionary of New Testament Words* under "LEAVEN"

LINE

Different words have this meaning: (1) *qāw*, a measuring line, 1 Kings 7:23; Jeremiah 31:39; especially the builder's measuring line, Zechariah 1:16, where God says He will stretch forth a line upon Jerusalem—that is, when the time comes for Him to show mercy to it. The same metaphor, however, is used for marking off that which is marked for destruction, for example, 2 Kings 21:13, where the line of Samaria and the plummet of the house of Ahab was to be stretched over Jerusalem. So in Isaiah 28:17, "I will make judgement the line" (R.V.) and 34:11, "the line of confusion." The word is used to signify a rule of life, that which goes by measurement. In Isaiah 28:10 the drunkards of Ephraim scoff at Isaiah's teaching as being "precept upon precept, line upon line" (as though he were teaching children their ABCs).

In Isaiah 44:13, KJV has "rule" (for a carpenter's instrument), R.V. has "line." In 18:2, 7, a double expression is used of Ethiopia, literally "a nation of line, line." This KJV translates "meted out," but the context rather confirms R.V. "that meteth out." A probable meaning is given by some by changing the word into one of very similar lettering, which gives the sense of "strong, strong."

In Psalms 19:4, "their line is gone out through all the earth," the line may signify their directing influences (as in KJV margin), tacitly exercising that which God has appointed for them and thus declaring His glory. This would not be inconsistent with the way in which the word is used in passages mentioned above. Perhaps, however, for *qawwām*, "their line" should be read *qôlām*, "their sound" or "voice," and this would seem to be borne out both by the parallel statement following, "their words to the end of the world," and by the fact that Paul applies the passage to the message of the Gospel in Romans 10:18, and uses the word "sound" (quoting the Septuagint). The two meanings are not dissociated, for each conveys the thought of the effect of God's declaration of His glory. (The suggestion of the sound of a stretched string is farfetched.)

(2) *ḥebel*, a cord or rope (one of its usual meanings), is rendered "line" (usually plural "lines") in 2 Samuel 8:2; Psalms 16:6, where the reference is to the portion marked off by a measuring cord (compare 105:11, "lot," margin, "cord"); Amos 7:17, of the dividing of Israel's land retributively.

(3) *ḥûṭ*, a thread or cord, is translated "line" in 1 Kings 7:15, of the measurement of the pillars.

(4) *pāthîl*, a lace, riband, or thread, is rendered "line"

in Ezekiel 40:3, of a line of flax, besides a measuring reed.

(5) *tiqwāh,* the usual meaning of which is hope or expectation, is used of the line of scarlet thread bound in the window by Rahab (Joshua 2:18, 21).

(6) *sered,* a pencil, is translated "line" in KJV of Isaiah 44:13 (R.V. "pencil," margin, "red ochre"), the only place where the word is used.

LOTS

The lot was used in Israel as a means of deciding urgent issues in cases where they were not left simply to the decision of a prophet, priest, elder, judge, or king. The adoption of lots presupposed that God controlled the matter and that the result was according to His will. This is clear from Proverbs 16:33. See also Joshua 18:6–8.

The circumstances in which decisions were so reached were various. Lots were used (1) in cases of wrongdoing, as in those of Achan (Joshua 7:14), the earliest instance; Jonathan (1 Samuel 14:42); Jonah (1:7), showing that the method was employed by others than Israelites; (2) in the assignment of property, as in the allocation of territory to the tribes of Israel (Numbers 26:55; 33:54; 34:13; 36:2; Joshua 13:6 and so forth; Psalms 125:3; see also Acts 13:19). The same word as used for casting lots (*gôrāl*) denotes the territory itself (for example, Joshua 15:1; Isaiah 57:6). Hence the term is applied metaphorically to signify a destiny appropriated by God, whether favorable or otherwise (Psalms 16:5; Isaiah 17:14; 34:17; Jeremiah 13:25; Daniel 12:13). Besides land, the division of booty or of the property of prisoners or those condemned to death was effected by lot (Psalms 22:18; Joel 3:3; Obadiah 11; Nahum 3:10); (3) in appointing to office or certain duties, as in the case of King Saul (1 Samuel 10:20), and in functions in the Temple worship (1 Chronicles 24:4, 5), or the service of song (1 Chronicles 25:8), or in providing wood for the altar (Nehemiah 10:34); (4) on the great Day of Atonement, when the lot was employed in choosing the he-goat for Jehovah and the one for Azazel (Leviticus 16: 7–10).

The actual method adopted in Israel in casting lots is not mentioned. Sometimes they were placed in the fold of the outer garment (Proverbs 16:33); compare the high priest's consultation of the Urim and Thummim. The custom has been entirely replaced by the guidance of the Spirit of God and the Word of God.

M

MANNA

Natural manna is the juice of the tarfa, a kind of tamarisk, and is chiefly found in Arabia. It is gathered from the leaves or twigs.

The supernatural manna described in Exodus was of an entirely different nature, and the evidences of its supernatural character are as follows: (1) it was found, not under the tamarisk tree, but on the surface of the ground in the wilderness, after the morning dew had disappeared; (2) it was found, throughout the forty years of Israel's journeyings, not during certain months in the year, but all the year round; (3) it ceased on the sabbath day; (4) the amount gathered on one day was greater than the natural amount produced per annum; (5) it could be ground and baked like meal; (6) it was not a mere juicy condiment, but was nutritious as bread; (7) a portion was kept in perpetuity in the ark. In this connection it may be noted that a probable derivation of the word is from Israel's question one to another, "[*man hû'*] *What is this?* For they knew not what it was" (Exodus 16:5 R.V.).

Everything about it is evidential of divine interposition and provision. For (*a*) there was no natural way of sustaining the nation in the wilderness; (*b*) God had divine purposes in maintaining His people in that manner, as it was through them that He would and will exercise

His governmental authority and provide salvation for
men; (c) there were spiritual facts analogical to natural
conditions.

For the description of it see Numbers 11:7–9. For allusions to it see Exodus 16:14–36; Deuteronomy 8:3–16;
Joshua 5:12; Psalms 78:24, 25; John 6:31–50; 1 Corinthians 10:3.

Certain spiritual lessons have been deduced from it:
(1) It was given freely: so with the Gospel and God's gift,
apart from works. (2) Each person was to gather according to his eating: so in regard to the needs of believers,
there is to be equality (2 Corinthians 8:14, 15), an avoid-
ance of mere luxury when others are in want. (3) It fell
from above: so Christ, the gift of God came from God the
Father, and is spiritually ministered day by day. (4) It
was gathered early: so the believer should receive his
spiritual food before the rush of daily circumstances begins. (5) It was ground in the mill: so Christ was bruised to
become our bread of life. (6) It was sweet to the taste: so
is God's Word to the believer. (7) It was to be gathered
day by day: so the believer needs fresh supplies of
spiritual food daily. (8) To the carnal "it was dry" food:
so is the Gospel to the worldling. (9) A part was preserved in the golden pot in the Holy of Holies (Hebrews
9:4; compare Exodus 16:33): so Jesus, now in the presence of God, provides hidden manna (Revelation 2:17),
unappreciated by the unbeliever. (10) It continued
throughout the wilderness journey: so Christ continues
with His people to the end of their course. (11) It ceased
when they reached the land: so faith will give place to
sight when the Lord brings His people to His eternal
rest.

MEAL OFFERING

This is the revised rendering of Hebrew *minhāh* for KJV "meat offering," except that in Jeremiah 14:12; 17:26; 13:18; 41:5, R.V. translates it "oblation," with "meal offering" in the margin. The laws of the "meal offering" (an offering never made with the blood of sacrifice) are given in Leviticus 2:1–16 and 6:14–23. The ingredients, flour and oil, were the usual vegetable foods of Israel; accordingly the Israelite offered in them his daily bread, but not as in the firstfruits of corn and bread (these latter were leavened and not burnt upon the altar, Leviticus 23:10–20); the meal offering was to contain no leaven and a portion was burnt on the altar for a sweet savour to Jehovah. The rest was eaten by the priests in the holy place, as the mediators between Jehovah and the people. Thus the meal offerings did not indicate merely the sanctification of earthly food, but set forth the spiritual food enjoyed by the Lord's people.

The Christian counterpart to the meal offerings has been recognized in the spiritual life provided in Christ, and nourished by the Holy Spirit (the oil) and the Word of God (the bread). This life must be free from the leaven of the old nature, the leaven of malice and wickedness, and from the honey of natural pleasures engaged in for mere self-indulgence (Leviticus 2:11). There must be salt as the purifying power of God's Word against moral corruption (verse 13) and the incense of prayer (verse 15).

MERCY, MERCIFUL

This word represents the following different Hebrew words:

(1) *hesedh,* which is sometimes rendered "loving-kindness"; it includes the qualities of kindly affection

and loyalty, for example, Psalms 77:8; 103:4, where it is coupled with and parallel to Number 2 (below) and Psalms 25:10; 26:3 (coupled with *'emeth*, fidelity) in Deuteronomy 7:9 (coupled with *berîth*, covenant). It is used of man towards man, for example, Judges 1:24, and is rendered "kindness" in the case of David and Jonathan (1 Samuel 20:14), but especially of Jehovah towards His people, for example, Genesis 19:19; 43:14; Psalms 5:7 (and very frequently in the Psalms).

(2) *raḥamîm*, literally, "bowels" and so, figuratively of compassion or tender affection. It is used of God towards man, for example, Nehemiah 1:11; Proverbs 14:21.

(3) the verb *ḥānan*, to show favor, to do kindness; it is rendered "be merciful" or "be gracious," "show mercy," "have pity," for example, Psalms 4:1; 6:2; 9:13 and is used of God towards man or of man towards man, for example, Proverbs 14:21, 31.

(4) *ḥemlāh* signifies to have compassion, Genesis 19:16, "the Lord being merciful unto him."

(5) *kāphar* (in the intensive form *kipper*) signifies to treat as forgiven, to forgive, as in Deuteronomy 21:8; 32:43, "be merciful."

MERCY SEAT

The Hebrew word *kappōreth* is connected with the verb *kipper*, to cover up or wipe out and hence to atone for offenses, to forgive. It was not a mere part of the ark. It was placed "above upon the ark" (Exodus 25:17–22; 26:34; 30:6; 31:7; 35:12; 37:6). It is never called "the cover of the ark" but is treated as something distinct. The Holy of Holies is called in two passages "the place of the mercy seat" (Leviticus 16:2; 1 Chronicles 28:11), making clear that it was more than a mere subordinate

part of the ark. The *kippûrîm*, that is, atonements, on the
Day of Atonement are connected inseparably with the
kappōreth, upon which the blood of the sin offering was
sprinkled. Accordingly the mercy seat covered that
which was inside the ark, namely the two tables of stone,
thus signifying that God in His mercy provided a propitiation for a breach of His covenant. By that means God
could speak to His people from above the mercy seat that
was upon the ark of the testimony from between the two
cherubim (Numbers 7:89); see also Psalms 80:1.

(For the New Testament word in Romans 3:25 and
Hebrews 9:5, see *Expository Dictionary of New Testament Words* under "MERCY-SEAT"; "PROPITIA-
TION.") The cherubim are indicative of the angelic
ministers of Jehovah, guardians in the attitude of adora-
tion. The throne of His earthly glory likewise represented the footstool of His heavenly throne.

MITRE

The so-called "mitre" was the headdress of the high
priest; the R.V. margin rightly has "turban" in Exodus
28:4, 37, 39; 29:6; 39:28, 31; Leviticus 8:9; 16:4; but in
Ezekiel 21:26 R.V. has "mitre," for the KJV "diadem."
This headdress was of fine linen, made from a piece said
to have been sixteen cubits long, rolled into the shape of
a turban; hence the name, *miṣnepheth* (from *ṣānaph*, to
wind). On the front was a plate of pure gold, on which
were graven, like the engravings of a signet, the words
signifying "Holy to Jehovah." This was put on a lace of
blue (gold and blue indicating glory and beauty respec-
tively, Exodus 28:2, 40). This was to be always on the
high priest's forehead that the children of Israel might
be "accepted before the LORD."

The turban represented the priestly dignity, just as the crown or diadem was of the royal. Hence in Ezekiel 21:26, "Remove the mitre [diadem]; and take off the crown" indicated the desolation of both priesthood and monarchy.

Another word, *ṣānîph*, from the same root is rendered "mitre" in KJV and R.V. of Zechariah 3:5 (R.V. margin "turban"). This the prophet saw on Joshua the high priest. In Job 29:14 (KJV "diadem," R.V. margin "turban") it is used figuratively of a righteous man clothed in the garments of nobility. In Isaiah 3:23 (KJV "hoods"; R.V. "turbans") it signifies an article of elaborate female attire. In Isaiah 62:3, it is a symbol of the honor which Jehovah will confer upon His people.

N

NEHUSHTAN

The word, signifying a bronze object (from *nehōsheth,* "bronze"), is found in 2 Kings 18:4 and the margin of R.V. defines it as a piece of brass. It was the contemptuous term given to the brazen serpent when Hezekiah broke it in pieces because it had been turned into an idol by the people. Israel had burnt incense to it, owing to its primary use in the typical miracle recorded in Numbers 21:8, 9.

NETHINIM

This word is connected with the verb *nāthan,* to give, and hence was the name for the servants of the Temple, as its slaves who were "given," to do the lowest menial work in connection with it. It is recorded in Ezra 8:20 that David and the princes "had appointed" the Nethinim "for the service of the Levites." These were no doubt the descendants of the captives taken at the close of the war against the Midianites. To the Levites, 320 captives (one out of every fifty) were given, and 32 to the priests (Numbers 31:40, 42, 47). Later, the Gibeonites were made by Joshua "hewers of wood and drawers of water for the congregation and for the altar of the Lord" (Joshua 9:27). In the first company that returned to Jerusalem under Zerubbabel (538 B.C.), there were 392 Nethinim and children of Solomon's servants (Ezra 2:43–58). Eighty years later, when Ezra was on his way

to Jerusalem he observed that in the company there
were few servants for the Temple. Accordingly he halted
to arrange for such to come from Casiphia and 220
Nethinim were sent to meet the need (Ezra 8:17–20). A
decree of Artaxerxes freed them from "tribute, custom or
toll" (7:24 R.V.). A list of these Nethinim is given in
Nehemiah 7:46–62. Those who dwelt in Jerusalem were
under the superintendence of two overseers, Ziha and
Gishpa (Nehemiah 11:21).

O

OATH

The word '*ālāh,* an oath, has more especially the sense
of a curse, as for example, in Numbers 5:21, 23, 27;
Deuteronomy 29:19, 20, 21; 30:7; Job 31:30; Psalms
10:7; Isaiah 24:6; Jeremiah 29:18; Daniel 9:11;
Zechariah 5:3. In Leviticus 5:1 the obligation to testify
when adjured, was fulfilled by the Lord when adjured by
Caiaphas (Matthew 26:63).

In Jewish criminal procedure, the accused was permit-
ted to clear himself or herself by oath (for example, 1
Kings 8:31).

The word *shebû'āh* (connected with *sheba',* seven, the
sacred number) denotes an oath, and is entirely so rendered (except in Isaiah 65:15 where it is translated "a
curse"). When an important agreement was entered into,
it was made binding by the parties to it subjecting themselves to an oath with due solemnity, as in the cases of
Isaac and Abimelech (Genesis 26:26–33), Joseph and the
Israelites (50:25), Rahab and the spies (Joshua 2:17–20),
Joshua and the Gibeonites (9:19, 20). An oath even to a
heathen king was so binding that because Zedekiah vio-
lated his oath to Nebuchadnezzar, God dethroned him
and gave him up to die in captivity (2 Chronicles 36:13).

For acts which accompanied the circumstances, see,
for example, Genesis 14:22; 24:2; 47:29; Leviticus 24:14;
Jeremiah 34:18.

The language used in the taking of or giving an oath

varies; the commonest expressions are "as the LORD liveth," "the LORD do so to me and more also." See also Genesis 31:53; 42:15. To violate an oath incurred a penalty, such as a curse, as in Numbers 5; Joshua 9 (hence the twofold meaning of *'ālāh*), and in view of the far-reaching consequences involved in the matter of an oath, the law imposed solemn restrictions in the case of members of a family other than the head (Numbers 30:1–15).

To appeal to a heathen god by oath was to acknowledge its deity, and therefore this was forbidden (Joshua 23:7; Jeremiah 5:7; 12:16; Amos 8:14). Swearing in appealing to God was to acknowledge Him (Deuteronomy 6:13; Isaiah 19:18; 65:16).

When God gave His promise on oath, those with whom He entered into relation had the assurance given them that His promise and His fidelity were unalterable. So with His word to Abraham, for example (Genesis 22:16–18; Psalms 105:9–11; compare Hebrews 6:13). In the case of Israel, such assurance placed them under an obligation to serve Him. For this reason His oath is adduced upon occasion; but not only so, with this were coupled the facts of His goodness in saving them, loving them, and giving them His Law.

(For the New Testament teaching on oaths see *Expository Dictionary of New Testament Words* under "OATH.")

OFFENCE, OFFEND

The English word "offend" in KJV has two meanings, (a) intransitively, to go astray, (b) transitively, to lead one astray. Hence an offence (offense) is either a trespass or the cause of a trespass, "a stumbling block."

The Hebrew words for "offence" are (1) *mikhshôl*,

used in 1 Samuel 25:31, "offence of heart" (KJV margin "stumbling"); in Psalms 119:165, the noun is translated "nothing shall offend them"; R.V. "they have none occasion of stumbling" (margin "They shall have no stumbling block"); in Isaiah 8:14 "a rock of offence"; (2) *heṭ'*—an error or sin, as in Ecclesiastes 10:4 "yielding allayeth great offences."

The following are Hebrew words for offend: (1) *'āsham*, or *'āshēm*, to be guilty, commit a trespass, for example, Jeremiah 2:3; 50:7; Ezekiel 25:12; Hosea 4:15; 13:1; Habakkuk 1:11. Thus Hosea 13:1, "when he offended in Baal he died" (R.V. margin "when he became guilty"); compare R.V. of Jeremiah 2:3 and Habakkuk 1:11. In 2 Chronicles 28:13, the noun *'ashmāh* is rendered "offend," as KJV "we have offended against the LORD"; R.V. "that which will bring upon us a trespass against the LORD." (2) *hāṭā* denotes to miss the way, hence, to sin against; as in Genesis 20:9, KJV "what have I offended thee?" (R.V. "sinned against"); 40:1; 2 Kings 18:14; Jeremiah 37:18. (3) *bāgadh* signifies to act treacherously as in Psalms 73:15; where KJV has "offend"; R.V. has "dealt treacherously with." (4) *hābhal* signifies to destroy, to spoil as in Job 34:31, "I will not offend any more" (New English Bible "I will do no more mischief"). (5) *pāshaʿ* signifies to rebel and so (in the passive) to take offence, as in Proverbs 18:19, "a brother offended [R.V. "injured"] is harder to be won than a strong city."

In the Septuagint the word *skandalon* translates the Hebrew word *môqēsh*, which denotes a bait and hence a snare (for the New Testament use of these words, see *Expository Dictionary of New Testament Words* under "OFFENCE," "OFFEND").

ORACLE

The common Hebrew term *dābār* ("word") frequently refers to the divine word or utterance of God, as by Urim and Thummim, or through a prophet, given for men's guidance (see 2 Samuel 16:23). The word *debîr*, frequently used in 1 Kings 6, has the meaning of the locality where such utterances were given, "the most holy place" of Solomon's Temple (6:16). The correct meaning of the Hebrew is found in Psalms 28:2, "I lift up my hands toward the innermost place of thy sanctuary" (R.V. margin).

The word "burden" (Hebrew *massā'*, a thing lifted up) is used, for example, in Nahum 1:1, signifying the burden of prophecy which was borne in upon the prophet when he received it from the Lord.

OUCHES

This English word was applied in KJV to gold ornaments, especially to a clasp or brooch set with jewels. The two jewels of onyx or beryl on the shoulders of the high priest were set in ouches (Hebrew *mishbeṣôth*) of gold (Exodus 28:11; 39:6 and so forth), a word derived from a root signifying to weave or wreathe. It is best represented in modern English by "filigree" work. The gold was beaten out into thin sheets, which were cut into narrow strips (39:3); thus they were formed into filigree as a setting to the jewels, and all were attached by gold thread to the ephod. Compare the ouches in Exodus 39:13 for the breastplate.

P

PAVILION

This word (derived from Latin *pāpiliō*, a butterfly, owing to the similarity in shape) is the translation of the word *sōkh* in Psalms 27:5, and of *sukkāh* in 2 Samuel 22:12 "pavilions"; it is rendered "tent" once, in 2 Samuel 11:11; see also 1 Kings 20:12, 16; Psalms 18:11; 31:20. In Job 36:29, R.V. has "pavilion" ("the thunderings of his pavilion") for KJV "tabernacles"; so in Isaiah 4:6 "there shall be a pavilion for a shadow in the daytime from the heat." The noun *sukkāh* is rendered "pavilion" in Psalms 18:11 and 31:20. It is frequently translated "tabernacles," especially in the phrase "the feast of tabernacles" (Deuteronomy 16:13, 16; 31:10; 2 Chronicles 8:13; Ezra 3:4; Zechariah 14:16, 18, 19). It is also frequently rendered "booths," for example, Leviticus 23:42, 43; "a booth" (Jonah 4:5); in Isaiah 1:8, R.V. "booth" for KJV "cottage."

The word *qubbāh* is found only in Numbers 25:8 (R.V. "pavilion" for KJV "tent"); it denotes the inner compartment of a tent. The word *shaphrûr* is found only in Jeremiah 43:10, where its meaning is given as "royal pavilion" (R.V. margin "glittering pavilion").

The royal pavilion was erected in the center of an army and it was surrounded by a constant guard of mighty men (compare Daniel 11:45 where *'appeden*, a word of Persian origin is used). The believer is protected and entertained by the sovereign power of almighty God (Psalms 27:5).

The word "pavilion" thus has sometimes the meaning of a temporary movable tent, sometimes that of a more permanent building.

PILLAR

(1) *maṣṣebeth* or *maṣṣēbāh*, from a root meaning to set upright, signifies any kind of upright stone. It is translated "pillar" in Genesis 35:14, 20; 2 Samuel 18:18 (it is rendered "substance" in Isaiah 6:13). (2) *neṣîb* (from the same root) is once rendered "pillar" (of salt), in Genesis 19:26 (the word commonly means "a garrison" as in 1 Samuel 13:3). (3) *ʿammûdh* (from *ʿāmadh*, "stand") is the usual word for pillar, and is of very frequent use; it signifies a column, and that is its meaning in Jeremiah 27:19.

The first of the above words has almost always a religious association and denotes the upright stone which accompanied the worship of the Israelites, and was the token of the divine presence. An offering of oil or of the blood of sacrifice was put upon it. The vision granted to Jacob at Bethel made that place a sacred spot, and there he set up a stone pillar and poured oil upon it (Genesis 28:18). Before the time of the captivity every sanctuary had its accompaniment of some such pillar or stone monument (Hosea 3:4, where the R.V. has "pillar" for KJV "image"). The following places are especially associated with the erection of a stone or pillar: Gilead (Genesis 31:45), Shechem (Joshua 24:26), Mizpeh (1 Samuel 7:12); here the stone gave the name to the spot, "Eben-ezer"; Gibeon (2 Samuel 20:8); En-rogel (1 Kings 1:9).

A pillar was reared by Absalom for himself in the king's dale, as he had no son to keep his name in remembrance, and he called the pillar after his own name; hence it became known as Absalom's place (2 Samuel 18:18). The prophecy concerning the future deliverance of Egypt in Isaiah 19:19–25, declares that there shall be an altar in the midst of the land "and a pillar at the border thereof to the LORD." Judges 9:6 states that the men of Shechem and all the house of Millo made Abimelech king "by the oak of the pillar [KJV margin; R.V. margin "terebinth"] that was in Shechem." This was a witness to the fact of his enthronement, in the place where he was acclaimed.

To set up a pillar as a stone symbol was forbidden (Deuteronomy 16:22 R.V. for KJV "image"). Yet despite this, stone pillars became objects of worship (Isaiah 57:6).

PILLOW

(1) The word *kebîr* is found only in 1 Samuel 19:13, 16. Michal put a pillow of goats' hair at the head of the teraphim she had laid in David's bed. The root from which the word is derived means to intertwine or to net; hence the meanings given in the R.V. margin, "quilt" or "network," one of which should probably be adopted. It was a quilt (Hebrew *makhbēr*) that Hazael used as a coverlet with which to smother Benhadad (2 Kings 8:15).

(2) The word *mera'ashāh* is translated "pillows" in KJV of Genesis 28:11, 18. The correct rendering is in R.V. "under his head." So in 1 Samuel 26:7, 11–16 (KJV "at his bolster"; R.V. "at his head"; compare verse 12, "from Saul's head"). The same word is used in 1 Kings 19:6.

(3) In Ezekiel 13:18, *keseth* is translated "pillows" in

KJV and R.V. The meaning probably is fillets or bands, used as amulets or charms, used for divination purposes.

PLEIADES

These are mentioned in three passages, Job 9:9; 38:31; Amos 5:8. In each place the Hebrew word *kîmāh* is used, which means a heap, which is the meaning of the Arabic word *kumat,* and is suggestive of the cumulative power of their influence. They are a group of stars, seven large and some small, in the constellation the Bull. In ancient times, the rising and setting of the group indicated the season of navigation. Hence the word is derived by most from the Greek verb *pleō,* to sail; others derive it (with less probability) from *pleōs,* full, owing to their appearance of being packed together.

In Job 9:9 and Amos 5:8 these constellations are shown to form part of that marvelous arrangement of Creation which bears testimony to the almightiness of the Maker. In Job 38:31 they are pointed out as signs of the seasons, the regular recurrence of which is utterly beyond the control of man. Man cannot bind the bands which hold this group of orbs together. The very purpose of God is that man's puny impotence should lead him to submit to Him: "Canst thou [with special emphasis on *thou*] bind the sweet influences of Pleiades?"

PLUMBLINE, PLUMMET

(1) *'eben,* a stone, is rendered "plummet" in the R.V. of Isaiah 34:11, margin "stones" (for KJV "stones"), indicating that a suspended stone was originally used as a plummet; the preceding clause "he shall stretch over it the line of confusion" (that is, measuring line) points to the R.V. rendering as to the use of a plumbline. In

Zechariah 4:10, the word definitely means a plummet; the full expression is, literally, "a stone of tin" (*bedhîl*) or possibly of reparation. The reference is to the rebuilding of the Temple, under Zerubbabel.

(2) *'anākh*, a plumbline is used only in Amos 7:7, 8 where it is used metaphorically of the measurement of judgment in the Lord's retributive dealings with Israel; the plumbline was represented as used, so to speak, in the construction of a wall as a witness (the Lord standing by the wall) to that which has not conformed to His will and word, and to the righteousness of the punishment to be executed upon the nation for its idolatry initiated by Jeroboam.

(3) *mishqōleth* is used in 2 Kings 21:13 of the plummet by which the house of Ahab has been tested, revealing his iniquities, and thus testing and revealing the iniquities of Manasseh and Judah, who followed the idolatrous ways of Israel in the north. A similar word, *mishqeleth*, is found in Isaiah 28:17, where the Lord says that He "will make judgment the line [that is, of measurement], and righteousness the plummet" (R.V.); that is, His righteousness will test and expose the lies under which the rulers of Jerusalem have hid themselves, in contrast to the "precious corner stone of a sure foundation" (verse 16, applied to Christ in 1 Peter 2:6).

PROGNOSTICATORS

These (Hebrew *môdhî'îm*) are mentioned in Isaiah 47:13 in the Lord's denunciation of Babylon. They are associated with the astrologers and the stargazers. They are described in the margin as those "that give knowledge concerning the months." The meaning of the last phrase probably is "at new moons," suggesting the forecasts which were customarily made at those seasons as to what was likely to happen during the ensuing month. The lucky and unlucky days of each month were noted in the Assyrian and Babylonian calendars, and reports were sent in monthly by official astrologers and astronomers.

The prophet Isaiah declares that none of them will avail to help Babylon in the approaching time of judgment. They themselves will be fuel for the flame which will consume them as stubble.

PROSELYTE

A proselyte (Hebrew $g\bar{e}r$) was originally one who took up his residence in a foreign land, putting himself under the protection of the people there; hence especially a foreigner residing in Palestine (Exodus 12:48; 20:10; 22:21; Leviticus 19:33). But later the word came to mean a foreign convert to the Jewish religion (for example, Matthew 23:15; Acts 2:10) and it ceased to signify merely residence in Palestine (see Acts 2:10 and 13:43).

Fixed conditions were laid down for "strangers" in Israel (for example, those who resided among Israelites, in the earlier sense of the word). The stranger was bound by the law of the sabbath (Exodus 20:10; 23:12; Deuteronomy 5:14). He must be circumcised before he ate the Passover (Exodus 12:48). He had to keep the Day of Atonement (Leviticus 16:29), and the Feasts of Weeks and of Tabernacles (Deuteronomy 16:11, 14). He was prohibited from eating blood (Leviticus 17:10) and from all the abominations of the Canaanites (18:24-30; 20:2), as well as from blasphemy (24:16). He could not hold land or intermarry with Aaron's descendants (so, by implication, Leviticus 19:10; 21:14).

He was to be treated kindly, in view of the fact that Israelites themselves were formerly strangers in Egypt (Exodus 22:21; 23:9; Leviticus 19:33, 34; Deuteronomy 10:18, 19). He was to share in the gleanings and tithes of the third year (Deuteronomy 14:29). He was to be treated with justice (Leviticus 24:22; Deuteronomy 1:16; 24:17, 19–21). He was regarded as in a subject condition; he was to assemble with Israel to hear the law read at the end of every seven years (Deuteronomy 31:10–12).

In times of judgment on the nation for departure from God, the stranger became superior to the Israelite; he became "the head" (Deuteronomy 28:43, 44). Under David and Solomon the strangers were subjected to bond service (1 Chronicles 22:2; 2 Chronicles 2:17, 18). In Esther's time many became Jews because "the fear of the Jews fell upon them" (8:17).

In the coming time of restoration foretold by the prophets, proselytes were to share in the blessings of Israel: "The strangers that join themselves to the LORD, to minister unto him, and to love the name of the LORD" shall be made joyful and their sacrifice will be accepted (see Isaiah 56:3–7).

Around the beginning of the Christian era some groups in Israel were engaged in an energetic campaign of proselytization among the Gentiles, with results which our Lord summed up in scathing terms (Matthew 23:15).

The expression "proselytes of the gate" was a rabbinical designation of resident aliens (as distinct from converts), derived from the reference in Exodus 20:10, and so forth, to "the stranger that is within thy gates."

Q

QUEEN OF HEAVEN

The queen of heaven was Astarte, the goddess of the planet Venus, called Ishtar by the Assyrians and Babylonians and Ashtoreth by the Phoenicians and other Canaanites. She was regarded as the sister or consort of Baal, the storm god. Together they were looked upon as symbolizing the generative powers of nature, and their worship is denounced in the Old Testament as abominable in the sight of Jehovah. Cakes were offered to the queen of heaven, drink offerings were poured out to her, and incense was burned in her honor (Jeremiah 7:18; 44:17–25). This idolatry became practiced in Judah and Israel, and in spite of the remonstrances and warnings of Jeremiah, his hearers strongly refused to listen to him and abandon their worship. They attributed their lack of plenty to the discontinuance of honor they paid to the goddess. Accordingly divine retribution upon them made Babylon, which had been a principal instrument of their idolatrous iniquity, the instrument of their punishment.

R

For RANSOM see REDEEM

For REDEEMER see KINSMAN

REDEEM, REDEMPTION

Two words in the Old Testament have the meaning to redeem. Hebrew *pādāh* is used of the payments required for the redemption of the firstborn (Exodus 13:13, 15; Leviticus 27:26, 27; Numbers 3:46–49; 18:15–17), or for the release of persons from slavery (Exodus 21:8; Leviticus 25:47–49). It is also used figuratively with the meaning of delivering, whether in the cases of individuals (Psalms 34:22) or of the deliverance granted to Israel as a nation (Deuteronomy 9:26; 2 Samuel 7:23; 1 Chronicles 17:21; Isaiah 29:22).

It is especially associated with the deliverance from Egypt (Deuteronomy 7:8; 13:5; 24:18; Micah 6:4). In one instance it is used of redemption from sin: "redeem Israel from all his iniquities" (Psalms 130:8).

The other verb is *gā'al* (with its active participle *gō'ēl*, for which see KINSMAN). It is used sometimes in the legal sense, of the recovery of property which had passed into other hands (Leviticus 25:26; Ruth 4:4, 7), or of the act of commuting a vow, the valuation of the offering being made by the priest (Leviticus 27:13, 15, 19, 20) or of the redemption of a part of a tithe (27:31).

Like *pādāh*, this word *gā'al* is used of God's deliver-

114

ances granted to Israel (Psalms 77:15; Isaiah 48:20; 52:3, 9) and especially of the coming deliverance of the nation from Gentile domination (Isaiah 35:9; 62:12; 63:4). It has been happily suggested that the use of these two words (rather than others which might have been chosen) is indicative of a relation between Jehovah and Israel, by way of His personal possession of them as His property. In this respect *pādāh* would lay stress on the purchase price, and *gā'al* would point to the kinsman side of the redemption. Moreover these two facts are brought out in the New Testament doctrine of redemption. Thus the Old Testament teaching, in various ways, foreshadows the acts of God's grace in His Son Jesus Christ in His becoming by His Incarnation our Kinsman and in the twofold aspect of His redemptive sacrifice, as a price paid and liberation accomplished on behalf of sinners, and as the deliverance wrought and yet to be consummated for believers.

Both words are used of deliverance from adverse circumstances: *pādāh* of deliverance from adversity itself (2 Samuel 4:9; 1 Kings 1:29; Psalms 25:22); *gā'al* of deliverance from oppression and violence (for example, Psalms 72:14); both words, of deliverance from captivity, *pādāh* in Zechariah 10:8–10; *gā'al* in Psalms 107:2, 3; both, of deliverance from death; *pādāh* in Job 5:20 and Psalms 49:15, *gā'al* in Psalms 103:4 and Hosea 13:14.

REFINE, REFINER

Two verbs are used with this meaning:

(1) *zāqaq* is used in a literal sense, of the refining of gold, Job 28:1, where R.V. has "a place for gold which they refine"; also in 1 Chronicles 28:18; of silver in 1 Chronicles 29:4; of settled wine, in Isaiah 25:6.

(2) *ṣāraph* is used in both the literal sense and in the metaphorical: literal in Psalms 66:10, "tried" (of silver); so in Zechariah 13:9; Jeremiah 6:29, "in vain do they go on refining [of lead]" (R.V.); metaphorical in Psalms 26:2, "try"; Isaiah 1:25, "purge"; 48:10, "I have refined thee"; Daniel 11:35, "to refine . . . them" (R.V.); in Malachi 3:2, 3, the word is rendered "refiner," where the Lord's purifying work is likened to a refiner's fire, when He sits "as a refiner and purifier of silver: and he shall purify the sons of Levi."

Gold was refined by being put into earthen crucibles with lead, salt, a little tin and barley bran, the crucibles being sealed with clay and then exposed to the heat of a furnace for five days and nights.

Silver was refined by being mixed with lead and put into a crucible made of bone earth, and placed in a furnace. The oxide of lead which formed was blown off by bellows, the effect being that the thin coating of lead became iridescent and disappeared, leaving the bright surface of silver. That process is referred to in Jeremiah 6:29. The crucible is called "the fining pot" (*maṣrēph*) Proverbs 17:3.

Affliction has a refining effect on the godly (1 Peter 1:7) but hardens the godless (Jeremiah 5:3). The Lord refines His elect till He sees His own image reflected in them (Job 23:10; Psalms 66:10; Isaiah 48:10; Hebrews 12:10).

Note: In Jeremiah 6:27 the true rendering is, "I have set thee for an assayer" (R.V., that is, refiner, separating the dross from the genuine metal).

ROD

Various meanings are attached to this word. It is

(1) an emblem of authority and power, as in the cases

of the rod of Moses (Exodus 4:2, and so forth), that of
Aaron (Exodus 7:10, 12 and so forth), those of the heads
of the tribes (Numbers 17:2–10); the Hebrew word is
maṭṭeh. In Genesis 49:10 and Judges 5:14, the word
shēbeṭ is translated "staff" in the R.V., and *maṭṭeh* is the
word for the sceptre, as an emblem of rule, in Ezekiel
19:11, 12, 14.

(2) an instrument of chastisement, 2 Samuel 7:14
("rod of men"); Job 9:34; 21:9; 37:13 (KJV margin, "a
rod," for text "correction"); so in Micah 6:9, "hear ye the
rod [*maṭṭeh*], and who hath appointed it." That is to say,
"listen to what God has to say in His disciplinary dealings." To do so is to receive restoring mercy. To hear the
rod is to realize and acknowledge the need of the chastisement. He who does so will be a "man of wisdom,"
learning "to walk humbly with his God" (verse 8).

(3) an instrument of divine retributive judgment in
the future upon the nations, Psalms 2:9; Isaiah 11:4 (Hebrew *shēbeṭ*). Compare Habakkuk 3:14, "staves" (Hebrew *maṭṭeh*).

(4) an emblem of travel or means of support, a staff.
Jacob, when setting out for Padan-aram left everything
behind except his staff (Genesis 32:10, Hebrew *maqqēl*).
The Israelites kept the Passover in Egypt each with his
staff in hand (Exodus 12:11). Balaam's staff (Numbers
22:27), with which he smote the ass, was ordinarily used
to support himself. David's staff (1 Samuel 17:40) was
what he ordinarily used in journeying, see also 2 Samuel
3:29 (*pelekh*). As a support in old age, see Zechariah 8:4
(*mish'eneth*).

(5) a shepherd's instrument of the defense of his flock
against animals and men, or for numbering the sheep as
they passed under the rod (Leviticus 27:32; Ezekiel

20:37 with Jeremiah 33:13). The rod was a club, about two and a half feet long, with a bulging head. It was either suspended by a thong from the shepherd's waistband, or inserted in a sheath or pocket in the outer cloak. Compare Micah 7:14 (margin "rule": the idea is that of tending the flock). The Hebrew word is *shēbet*.

(6) a shepherd's instrument for guiding, caring for and dealing with his sheep. This (Hebrew *mish'eneth*) was a straight pole about six feet long; it was used for beating leaves from branches out of the reach of sheep, or for support while climbing, or for leaning upon and inspiring his flock with confidence. The primary meaning of *mish'eneth* is something upon which to lean. In this connection the word is used in Isaiah 36:6, of the unreliability of Egypt as the "staff" of a bruised reed for Israel to lean upon.

(7) an emblem or representation of the supernatural power of the angel of the Lord (Judges 6:21, "staff") or that given by God to a prophet as in the case of Elisha's staff (2 Kings 4:29), Hebrew *mish'eneth*.

(8) figurative of an oppressor (Isaiah 9:4, "rod"; 10:5, 15, 24; 14:5, "staff") (Hebrew *matteh* and *shēbet*).

(9) a flail for beating out fitches and a rod for a similar purpose (Hebrew *matteh* and *shēbet*).

(10) an instrument for digging a well (Hebrew *mish'eneth*, Numbers 21:18, "staves").

(11) the strength of a nation, for example, Moab, Jeremiah 48:17, "staff" (*matteh*) and rod (*maqqēl*).

(12) a twig or shoot, used in Isaiah 11:1 with reference to Christ's Incarnation and development (R.V. "shoot" or KJV "rod"); the figure is that of a cut-down stump (the nation of Israel) which would put forth a single flourishing shoot (Hebrew *hōter;* the only other place where this

word is used is in Proverbs 14:3) (KJV "a rod of pride";
R.V. margin "shoot").

(13) an instrument of divination by rhabdomancy,
practiced by apostate Israel (Hosea 4:12, "staff," Hebrew
maqqēl).

(14) the sceptre of Messiah's coming sovereignty
(Hebrew *matteh*, Psalms 110:2, "the rod of thy
strength"); compare Micah 7:14.

S

SACKCLOTH

This was a coarse material (Hebrew *saq*) woven from either goats' hair or camels' hair, and was dark in color as indicated in Isaiah 50:3 in the figurative expression regarding the clouds of heaven; compare Revelation 6:12.

To put on sackcloth was a sign of sorrow and mourning (Genesis 37:34; 2 Samuel 3:31; 21:10; 1 Kings 21:27; 2 Kings 6:30; 19:1, 2; 1 Chronicles 21:16; Nehemiah 9:1; Esther 4:1–4; Job 16:15; Psalms 35:13; 69:11; Lamentations 2:10) of repentance (Jonah 3:5, 6, 8) or of humiliation and subjection, as an appeal for pity to superiors (1 Kings 20:31, 32). It was the accompaniment of fasting in self-judgment and in intercession (Isaiah 58:5; Daniel 9:3).

In the following passages, warnings were given to wear it in repentance (Isaiah 22:12; Jeremiah 4:8; 6:26; 49:3). In the following passages future judgments are foretold and conditions involving the wearing of sackcloth (Isaiah 3:24; 15:3; Ezekiel 7:18; 27:31; Joel 1:8, 13; Amos 8:10).

To put it off or have it removed was indicative of joy in relief from sorrow (Psalms 30:11). In Isaiah 20:2, the Lord commanded Isaiah to put off the outer garment of sackcloth, to indicate that Egypt would be stripped of its possessions, and to give a silent exhortation as to the need of repentance.

SATYR

The Hebrew word *sā'îr* (plural *se'îrîm*) primarily meant a he-goat. In lower Egypt the goat was worshiped with abominable rites. The word is rendered "satyr" in two passages, Isaiah 13:21 and 34:14 (R.V. margin "he-goat"). In both places the Septuagint translates it *daimonia*, demons, and this gives the true indication of the evil spirits which inspired the particular worship carried on by the idolaters: "the things which the Gentiles sacrifice, they sacrifice to demons and not to God" (1 Corinthians 10:20). The word is translated "devils" (that is, demons) in KJV Leviticus 17:7 "they shall no more offer their sacrifices unto devils, after whom they have gone a whoring" (R.V. "he-goats"; margin "satyrs"), that is, to the evil spirits. The same rendering is given in the margin of 2 Chronicles 11:15. Here the Septuagint translates it *mataia*, vain things.

SCAPEGOAT

On the Day of Atonement the high priest presented two goats before the Lord at the door of the Tabernacle (Leviticus 16), and cast lots upon them: one was "for Jehovah," the other "for Azazel." For the sacrifice of the former, see verses 15–19. The high priest laid his hands on the goat "for Azazel," confessing the sins of the people. Then a man, chosen for the purpose, led it into the wilderness and let it loose (indicating the complete removal of the sin of the people of God, so that no witness can rise in judgment against them). In Leviticus 16:10, 26, the rendering should be "the goat for the complete sending away"; the root *'āzal* means "to remove completely."

Some have thought that Azazel signifies the devil, as

the source of sin, and thus the removed one in the wilderness, the abode of evil spirits. But this goat, like the other, was presented before Jehovah as being consecrated to Him (verse 7). The two together have been interpreted as typifying two aspects of the one sacrifice of Christ, the goat for Azazel typifying the effect of His sacrifice, in that Christ, who was sacrificed "for our offences," was "raised for [on account of] our justification" (Romans 4:25), that is, because our justification had been completed by His offering. Life as the result of His death is therefore indicated in Azazel.

SCEPTRE

A sceptre is the rod or staff of a ruler, especially of a sovereign, but also of other chief potentates. Thus Isaiah 14:5 speaks of "the sceptre of the rulers." The earliest mention of a sceptre in Scripture is in Genesis 49:10, which prophesies that Judah is to be the permanent sphere in which Messiah's sovereign power will be exercised; "unto him shall the obedience of the peoples be" (R.V.); see Isaiah 11:10 R.V. There were two forms of a sceptre, one a short ornamental one, the other a long staff ornamented at its upper end. Both are apparently in view here, the former (*shēbeṭ*) being the sceptre, the latter *meḥōqēq* the "ruler's staff" (R.V). Balaam prophesied that "a sceptre [*shēbeṭ*] shall rise out of Israel." Here again both sceptre and star are symbolical of the coming sovereign rule of Christ. In Psalms 45:6 Messiah's sceptre (*shēbeṭ*) is used to indicate the righteous character of His rule: "A sceptre of equity is the sceptre of thy kingdom" (Hebrew 1:8). The staff (*maṭṭeh*) and the sceptre (*shēbeṭ*) of the oppressive rulers of Babylon and associated powers at the time of restoration are to be broken by divine action (Isaiah 14:5, 6).

In Ezekiel 19:11 the prophet laments the fact that whereas Israel as a vine once had "strong rods for the sceptres of them that bare [bear] rule," destruction had come upon her, her strong rods were broken off and withered, and there was now "no strong rod to be a sceptre to rule." The strong rods were the princes of the house of David. The vine shot forth her branches like sceptres. In Amos 1:5 the Lord, foretelling the punishment of Damascus, says He will cut off "him that holdeth the sceptre" (here and Ezekiel 10 the Septuagint translates the word *shēbet* by its other meaning "tribe," Greek *phulē*). In Zechariah 10:11 the sceptre of Egypt is doomed; that is, there would be none to rule there.

In Esther 4:11; 5:2; 8:4, a slightly different form (of Aramaic origin) is used for the sceptre of Ahasuerus (*sharbît*).

In Numbers 21:18 R.V. corrects KJV "by direction of the lawgiver" to "with the sceptre." So in Psalms 60:7 and 108:8, "Judah is my sceptre" (margin "lawgiver," as in KJV). In Psalms 125:3, R.V. rightly has "the sceptre of wickedness" for KJV "the rod of the wicked."

SELAH

This word is used seventy-one times in the Psalms and three times in Habakkuk. It is probably connected with *sālal*, to lift up, said of the instruments, to increase the sound, while the voice is silent (or perhaps a call to the voice to sound), or (less probably), with *shālāh*, to rest, indicating either the pause of the voice in singing so that only instruments were heard, or a break in the psalm where there is a call to rest and reflect on the preceding words. In Psalms 9:16 it follows the word *higgaion*, which means meditations, as in its use in Psalms 19:14. The word is never used at the beginning of a psalm, nor has it any grammatical connection with the context. Its usual position is either at the end of a strophe or at the end of a psalm. Four times it is found in the middle of a verse: Psalms 55:19; 57:3; Habakkuk 3:3, 9.

It often connects what precedes with what follows (sometimes by way of contrast), so as to stress both, as if saying, "This being so, give heed to what is now to be said." Its connecting significance may be seen in linking one psalm with another, as in Psalms 3 and 4.

SERAPHIM

These are an order of heavenly beings, mentioned in Isaiah 6:2, 3. The word has been taken to mean bright or shining, but the verb *sāraph* means to burn, and the root has the transitive sense of consuming with fire (as when it is used adjectively of the "fiery" serpents of Numbers 21:6), and not glowing with heat. The sixth verse confirms this, where one of the seraphim takes "a live [that is, hot] coal" from the altar, and touches the prophet's mouth with it, saying, "Lo, this hath touched thy lips; and thine iniquity is taken away, and thy sin purged." The altar was the altar of burnt offering in the Temple court, the fire on which consumed "the burnt offering and the fat," when the glory of the Lord appeared to all the people (Leviticus 9:23). It was the glory of the Lord that caused Isaiah to acknowledge his own sinfulness, in contrast to the utterances of the seraphim, crying one to the other, "Holy, holy, holy, is the LORD of hosts."

Each seraph has face, hands, and feet, indicating that they are not merely mystical beings, but are possessed of powers which are used to do God's will. Each has three pairs of wings, one pair being used to veil their faces, as being unworthy to look on God; another pair is used to cover their feet, as being in an attitude of waiting upon God to carry out His behests; the third is used for the rapid activity of fulfilling that for which they are sent. Thus they differ from the cherubim in Ezekiel 10, and the living creatures in Revelation 4:8.

SHEOL

Three distinct words are rendered "hell" in KJV. The R.V. is more exact. The Hebrew word *She'ol*, for example, in Deuteronomy 32:22 (R.V. "the lowest pit"), is probably derived from a root "to make hollow," and was seen as the common receptacle of the dead, below the earth. Sheol signifies depth in Job 11:8 (R.V.) and insatiability in Isaiah 5:14. "If I make my bed in hell [R.V. Sheol], behold, thou art there" (Psalms 139:8) shows it as a place to which the power of God extends. It is rendered "the grave" in Song of Solomon 8:6, signifying cruelty.

For the two words Hades and Gehenna (translated "hell" in the New Testament) see *Expository Dictionary of New Testament Words* under "HADES," "HELL."

For SHEWBREAD see *Expository Dictionary of New Testament Words* under "SHEWBREAD"

SHOE

The wearing of shoes or sandals was a symbol of journeying by foot (Exodus 12:11); compare the action of the Gibeonites in Joshua 9:5, 13, in pretending that they had been on a long journey.

In the Oriental life of peasants and others, dust-covered or mud-stained shoes were left at the door of the house, when about to enter.

When approaching the presence of God, the recognition of being on holy ground was necessary and was to be indicated by the removal of the shoes, as in the command to Moses (Exodus 3:5), to Joshua (Joshua 5:15); compare Isaiah 20:2.

The shoe of witness is mentioned in two passages. In Deuteronomy 25:9, 10, the husband's brother permits the widow to take off his sandal, and she reproaches him by word and act for refusing to undertake a privilege and duty. The possession of one shoe by the widow was like a bill of divorce, setting her free to marry another, while the retention of the other shoe by the man was his covering proof that all claims had been formally settled.

Ruth 4:7, 8 shows that it was the custom when property was sold or any right given up, to take off the sandal and hand it to the purchaser or to the person to whom the right was transferred. It was thus a witness as to the legal completion of the negotiations.

A different significance attaches to the statement in Psalms 60:8 and 108:9, "over Edom will I cast out my shoe." Possibly the allusions to Edom and Moab are contemptuous, Edom being regarded as a place into which dirty shoes may be cast. Some suggest that Edom is regarded as a slave to whom his master tosses his sandals. Another possible significance is that the casting of the shoe on a land is a legal symbol, indicating a claim to ownership, and hence of taking possession.

In Deuteronomy 33:25, R.V. rightly has "bars" for the KJV "shoe."

For SIMILITUDE see IMAGE

SIN OFFERING

The sin offerings for sins committed through ignorance were as follows: for a ruler, a he-goat (Leviticus
4:25); for an ordinary person, a she-goat, a ewe-lamb, a
turtle dove or young pigeon, or a cereal (4:29, 32; 5:7,
11); for priests (4:3), for Levites at their installation
(Numbers 8:8), and for the whole congregation
(Leviticus 4:14), a bullock and for the last mentioned a
he-goat (Numbers 19:2–4). On the Day of Atonement a
bullock was offered for the high priest and he-goats for
the congregation (Leviticus 16:3 and so forth). The details of the offerings are given in chapters 4 and 5.

The similar offerings in the new commonwealth of
Ezekiel 43–45 are not by way of atonement for sins of
ignorance but for the consecration of holy places.

To be distinguished from the sin offering is the trespass or guilt offering. This was for unwitting trespass
against God's ordinances in regard either to holy things
(Leviticus 5:15) or to the rights of property (chapter 6),
reparation was required for the trespass with the addition of a fine one-fifth of the value of the thing to be
restored, which went to the priest (5:16). Where the injury was a private wrong, restitution had to be made to
the injured party; if there were no kinsmen, it went to
the priest; the victim was usually a ram (Numbers 5:7, 8).
In one respect the sin offering differed from the guilt
offering in that the former was required where the harm
done could not be undone or measured.

In Isaiah 53:10, "when thou shalt make his soul an
offering for sin," the Hebrew word is *'āshām*, a guilt
offering.

The guilt offering covered five distinct forms of trespass (Leviticus 5:6; 6:2; 14:12; 19:21; Numbers 6:12) all

of which represented a wrong for which a special ransom was given. That a trespass offering was ordered in the case of a healed leper, and in that of a Nazirite whose vow had been interrupted by contamination with the dead, was no exception. The former's infection worked against the congregation, the latter's against the Lord.

The Hebrew word for sin offering is the same as that for sin (*hattā'th*); the word for trespass offering is the same as that for trespass (*'āshām*). The former relates to personal condition, the evil nature, the latter to the effects, evil action.

For SPIKENARD see *Expository Dictionary of New Testament Words* under "SPIKENARD"

For STRANGER see PROSELYTE

T

TACHES

These were golden clasps, fifty in number, attached at equal distances along one set of curtains in the Tabernacle, fitting into the same number of loops along the edge of the second set, coupling the two sets together. The command to Moses was, "Thou shalt make fifty taches of gold, and couple the curtains together with the taches: and it shall be one Tabernacle" (Exodus 26:6).

In addition to these, there were fifty taches (clasps) of bronze, under which was the veil, which divided the holy place from the Holy of Holies.

TERAPHIM

These are supposed to have originally been household gods (compare Genesis 31:19; 1 Samuel 19:13, 16). The most frequent mention of them in the Old Testament shows that they were associated with the practices of magic and soothsaying. The Syriac *teraph* means to enquire of an oracle. The Arabic *tarafa* means to enjoy the things of life. In the following places the word has been left untranslated: in the R.V. of Genesis 31:19, 34; 1 Samuel 15:23; 19:13, 16; 2 Kings 23:24; Ezekiel 21:21; Zechariah 10:2 (for KJV "images" or "idols"). Both versions have it untranslated in Judges 17:5; 18:14, 17, 18, 20; Hosea 3:4, in all of which it is associated with an idolatrous ephod. While they were used in idolatrous worship, they were also used for purposes of divination and are mentioned together with those who consult familiar spirits and wizards, in 2 Kings 23:24 (so in Ezekiel 21:21 and Zechariah 10:2), and to obtain good luck for a house. The Israelites in their apostasy from God combined both these purposes with the worship of Jehovah.

TIRSHATHA

This was the official title of the governor of a province under the Persian rule. The word is derived from a Persian root signifying "his severity," as if conveying powers of the strictest administration. Such was the authority given to the governor of Judea. It was applied to Zerubbabel (Ezra 2:63; compare Nehemiah 7:65, 70; Haggai 1:1; 2:2) and to Nehemiah (Nehemiah 8:9; 10:1; 12:26). The appointment was made by the king, and usually the Tirshatha acted as a commissioner or plenipotentiary, invested with the powers of a viceroy, sent on a special mission on the accomplishment of which his appointment terminated.

U

URIM and THUMMIM

The meanings of these words are "lights" and "perfections." When mentioned together their distinctness is indicated by the use of the article before each. They were in the breastplate of the high priest when he went in before the Lord "into the holy place" that he might "bear the judgment of the children of Israel upon his heart before the Lord continually" (Exodus 28:30). The judgment was all that lies in the counsels and decisions of God concerning His people. In Deuteronomy 33:8 the order is "thy Thummim and thy Urim," suggesting that in the blessings promised to Levi, the divine lights are the effects of the manifestation of the divine perfections. It was the responsibility of the successors of Aaron still to guide the people by making inquiry from God and receiving the answer through the Urim. The leadership of Joshua became established in this way. He was to be set before Eleazar, the priest, who would inquire for him by the judgment of the Urim before the Lord (Numbers 27:21). Here the Urim is mentioned without the Thummim. Joshua's authority over the people was thus dependent upon the lights which God could alone supply. A good example of the use of Urim and Thummim is provided in the complete text of 1 Samuel 14:41 according to the Septuagint (something has fallen out of the Hebrew text in the course of transmission).

The last priest recorded as using the ephod and its

Urim and Thummim was Abiathar (1 Samuel 23:6–9). At the close of King Saul's career, God refused to answer his inquiry, "whether by dreams, or by Urim or by prophets" (28:6). Reference is made in Ezra 2:63 and Nehemiah 7:65, to an indefinite time when possibly a priest should again stand up "with Urim and with Thummim," but there is no documented instance after the time of David. Later revelations of the mind of God came through the prophets. The judgment of God now centers in His Son, to whom at His right hand He has committed all authority, and the will of God is given to believers in the completed and all sufficient Scriptures of truth, ministered by the Holy Spirit.

W

WEEPING

Weeping (Hebrew *bākhāh*) is frequently mentioned in Scripture as a natural expression of grief and mourning; compare the place name Bochim in Judges 2:5. It is also connected with fasting, as in 2 Samuel 1:11, 12; 12:21; Psalms 69:10, and with the rending of garments, for example, 2 Kings 22:19. Weeping accompanied national repentance of sin by the people, see Ezra 10:1.

The valley of Baca, in the neighborhood of Jerusalem, represented a place of spiritual drought and dejection, the only water being that of "tears." Hence travelers "passing through the valley of Weeping they make it a place of springs" (Psalms 84:6 R.V.). It therefore symbolized a place of ever-flowing comfort, a "highway to Zion" (verse 5 R.V.). Perseverance and trust not only overcome difficulties but turn them into blessings.

WELL

A well (Hebrew *be'ēr*) is dug, whereas a fountain (Hebrew *'ayin, ma'yān*) is a natural spring. But in KJV the word "fountain" is often used to describe a well. Many wells were important as landmarks, and as valuable possessions, see Deuteronomy 6:11. They were often a cause for rejoicing, as in Numbers 21:17, 18, when "Israel sang this song, Spring up, O well; sing ye unto it: The princes digged the well, the nobles of the people digged it."

The earliest mention of wells in the Old Testament is in Genesis 16, in connection with Hagar when she fled into the wilderness. The well which Abraham dug at Beer-sheba (21:30) had been a place of strife; it marked the place of covenant between himself and Abimelech. Another was at Haran (see chapter 29), and was the meeting place of Jacob and Rachel. The twelve wells at Elim (Exodus 15:27), also referred to as "fountains" in Numbers 33:9, gave the children of Israel a place of much-needed refreshment, after experiencing the bitter waters of Marah. The well at the gate of Bethlehem, for whose waters David thirsted in 1 Chronicles 11:17, may have been a pit or cistern (Hebrew $b\bar{o}r$).

For WITCHCRAFT see DIVINATION

Y

YOKE

In Scripture the word "yoke" is chiefly used in connection with the plough. The pair of beasts in ploughing is called a yoke, for example, in 1 Samuel 11:7 (ṣemedh, a pair); of asses (Judges 19:3); 1 Kings 19:19; Job 1:3; a couple of horsemen (Isaiah 21:7). In Isaiah 5:10, ṣemedh is translated "acres," that is, the amount of land a yoke of cattle could plough in a day (literally "yokes").

Metaphorically, the yoke was the emblem of subjection and servitude (Genesis 27:40; Leviticus 26:13; 1 Kings 12:4; Lamentations 3:27; Nahum 1:13). In the case of exceptionally severe subjection the yoke was described as consisting of iron (Deuteronomy 28:48; Jeremiah 28:14).

To impress the Jewish people with the necessity of submitting quietly to Nebuchadnezzar, Jeremiah put a yoke on his own neck, which he wore in public. Hananiah, a popular prophet who cried, "Peace, peace," when there was no peace, tore the yoke off Jeremiah's neck to back up his own prediction that within two years God would break off from the nation the eastern monarch's yoke. To this Jeremiah was appointed to reply, "Thus saith the LORD: Thou hast broken the yokes of wood, but thou shalt make for them yokes of iron. For thus saith the LORD of hosts, the God of Israel: I have put a yoke of iron upon the neck of all these nations, that they may serve Nebuchadnezzar king of Babylon" (Jeremiah 28:10–14).

APPENDIX

Historical Comparisons

Formation	Deliverance	Wanderings	Conquering	Declension	Saul	David	Division	Captivity	Exile	Temple	City	Silent	Christ	Church	Completion
Genesis	Exodus	Numbers	Joshua	Judges	1 Samuel	2 Samuel	1 Kings	2 Kings	Daniel	Ezra	Nehemiah	years	Gospels	Acts	1 Timothy through Revelation

2000 B.C.   1500   1000   722   606   536   400   6 B.C.   A.D. 32   A.D. 66   A.D. 100

Abraham   Moses   Saul David Solomon   Assyria   Babylon   End of Old Testament

Temple

Birth of Christ   Death of Christ   Death of Paul   Death of John

Genesis	Exodus	Numbers	Joshua	Judges	1 Samuel	2 Samuel	1 Kings	2 Kings	Daniel	Ezra	Nehemiah	Silent	Gospels	Acts	Completion
Job	Leviticus	Deuteronomy		Ruth		Psalms	Song of Solomon, Proverbs, Ecclesiastes	Note 1	Ezekiel	Esther, Haggai, Zechariah	Malachi	years	Matthew, Mark, Luke, John	Note 2	Note 3

——— 1 - 2 Chronicles ———

Note 1. Isaiah, Jeremiah, Lamentations, Hosea, Joel, Amos, Obadiah, Jonah, Micah, Nahum, Habakkuk, and Zephaniah.

Note 2. Romans, 1-2 Corinthians, Galatians, Ephesians, Philippians, Colossians, 1-2 Thessalonians, Philemon, Hebrews, James.

Note 3. 1-2 Timothy, Titus, 1-2 Peter, 1-3 John, Jude, Revelation.

(From *Let's Know the Bible* by John W. Cawood)

HOW, WHEN AND BY WHOM WAS THE BIBLE WRITTEN

James Todd, D.D.

When Was the Bible Written?

And the Lord said unto Moses, Write thou these words.

Exodus 34:27

Sir Walter Scott on his death bed said to Lockhart, his friend, "Bring me the book." In reply, Lockhart asked, "What book?" But though Scott was a genius who knew most books, he answered, "Lockhart, there is only one book—the Bible."

It is this book of which I propose giving a brief account—this book, whose disciples, with a few exceptions, form the empire of genius, the realm of intellect, and the fabric of morals and religion—the book acknowledged by the greatest minds to be the best book in the best age of the world's history.

When, how, and by whom, did mankind receive this Bible?

THE BIBLE AS HISTORY

The Bible consists of a collection of sixty-six books, thirty-nine in the Old, and twenty-seven in the New Testament. The large preponderance of recognized writers on this question tell us the Old Testament books were given to the world during a period of fifteen hundred years before Christ. But it is almost beyond question that the Book of Job was written at a much earlier date. At the dawn of Israelite history, Abraham was called to go forth from his Chaldean home to the Promised Land of his age, and with the going forth of this patriarch began the writing of this Bible.

The historical portions of the book form, in large part, a history of the Israelites in their relations to God, and to the nations with whom they came into contact. It was not, however, a final and complete history of those relations, but one in process of development, which pointed to a future and fuller unfolding of them. It is such a history of man in the family, of man in the nation, of man in the wider sphere of the world; a history with its universal application for all time to man, in all his relationships of human life. Hence the development of this history must be coextensive with human experience, and the progress of its truth may be as great as the march of thought without occasioning any surprise in the minds of the most devout believers.

Abraham was the principal founder of these relations of which the Old Testament is in such large part a history. Indeed, so strongly is this thought emphasized in the Bible that he is called "the Father of God's Faithful." Therefore the reasonableness of Abraham's writing his own family history in an intelligible (though it may be an abbreviated) form can hardly be rationally gainsaid.

The authorship of the first five books of the Bible is, we believe, accurately ascribed to Moses, but there is no reasonable doubt that Moses used in his writings all the necessary material which history had placed at his disposal.

Indeed, such material available for both Moses and Abraham must have been very considerable. For, whether the deluge was universal or local in its extent, whether the Babel of tongues was natural or supernatural, whether the overthrow of Sodom and Gomorrah was miraculous or not, that these things occurred somehow is *a matter of history apart from the Bible narrative.* The excoriated landscape still visible around that valley of Sodom, the universal testimony given by expert geologists, and the imperishable stone and other writings of nations contemporaneous with these people prove these narratives historical by whomever they were written. By these facts, the historic character of even the pre-Mosaic portions of the Bible is verified, their literary sources revealed, and the time when they were written.

It is sometimes objected that the peoples of those days were too primitive to know the art of writing, but long before the days of Abraham, those eastern people from whence he came had attained a very creditable state of civilization.

It is unreasonable to suppose that in such a condition of society Abraham was ignorant of this art. He was the appointed patriarch of a believing race, and the principal incidents in his life, which was so noble and was designed to be the uplifting force of his generation, naturally would be compiled and recorded by competent hands to teach the unborn hosts. That this was done is suggested in the command to Moses "to write this for a memorial in a book" (Exodus 17:14). This "memorial" book was doubtless the historic record of God's dealings with Israel since the call of Abraham, and we read that Moses commanded that those records be continued.

As the material accumulated, it would become necessary to condense the writings, and narrate only the most important events. Also those incidents relating more especially to the religious life of the people would naturally find a place in such a book. For in this Bible, as the history of man develops, religion is shown to be the soul of history, the central power in the affairs of the nation, the deepest foundation of human life. Doubtless the necessary abridgement of the narratives accounts to some extent for the Mosaic legislation being recorded piecemeal, and mingled with the history of the wilderness period.

A careful reading of the five books of Moses reveals that they were largely written as the history was made, and not as history is usually written—long after the fact. Much of the ceremonial legislation for those people was passed to suit their immediate needs. As a proof of this, one eminent naturalist has observed that the list of clean and unclean beasts contained in the fourteenth chapter of Deuteronomy mentions nine different animals which are not referred to in the parallel passage in Leviticus. Six of these are animals still to be found in the wilderness, and in the eastern plateau, and could never have been inhabitants of the hilly, wooded, and cultivated Western Palestine, nor of Egypt. They are birds exclusively of the desert open plain, or of bare rocky heights, and were added to the list mentioned in Deuteronomy after they had been met with in the wilderness, and many years journeyings there had made the Israelites familiar with them.

Sir William Dawson pointed out that the Book of Exodus is an Egyptian book, which contains numerous words and phrases descriptive of Egyptian manners, and colored with Israelite ideas of desert life. For example, the plagues narrated in the Book of Exodus are nearly all natives of the climate and soil of Egypt. It is plain that the golden calf set up at the foot of Mount Sinai by the rebellious Israelites is Egyptian, and was made in imitation of the Egyptian deity—Apis. If we observe the references of the writer to the Pharaohs, to the Nile whose waters were turned into blood, if we think upon these revelations of Egyptian tyranny and civilization, we believe common sense—without either scholarship, or religious faith—compels us to decide that in this book we have an account of a forced exodus of people from lower Egypt when that country was in a high state of civilization and prosperity. Indeed, so real is the narrative that one of the strongest opponents to the inspiration of the Bible admits that it contains nothing which does not correspond with the court of Pharaoh. Thomas Huxley himself said, "The Book of the Exodus is the best guidebook to Egypt." Now, if we can find the time when the exodus from Egypt took place, we can tell when the first five books of our Bible were given to us. This may be done approximately, though the exact time cannot be stated with absolute certainty.

WHEN WAS THE EXODUS?

There is the strongest possible evidence that the Hyksos—the Shepherd kings of Egypt—reigned in the time of Abraham. Manetho, an ancient, yet a reliable

Egyptian historian, informs us that these kings reigned for a little over two centuries, and were succeeded by the eighteenth succession or dynasty of native Egyptian kings. Soon after this, Joseph, the Hebrew, came to Egypt, and Jacob, his father, and his family, settled there in the time of Thothmes III, one of the greatest kings of that succession. A revolution soon afterwards occurred which resulted in introducing a new dynasty of which Rameses I and Rameses II were the earliest kings. These were the kings or Pharaohs who "knew not Joseph." They were the Napoleons of Egypt and powerful oppressors of the subject races. Maneptah succeeded Rameses II, and according to a papyrus account, there occurred at that time a great exodus from Egypt which was followed by national anarchy. Therefore, it is almost certain that the Pharaoh named Siptah Maneptah, otherwise spoken of as Amenophis (or Merenptah), was the ruler when the Israelites left Egypt, in the thirteenth century B.C. It is also as certain that the Exodus took place sometime during the four short reigns which succeeded that of Rameses II, and that the five books of Moses were written about 1300 years before Christ.

Indeed, if we are to have a historical basis for the Scriptures, it would be very difficult, if not impossible, to find another period of time—other than the wilderness years of these Israelites—when the Mosaic and Levitical legislation could have been appropriately enacted for, and imposed upon, these people, with either reason or effective purpose.

And just as these writings were begun, so were they continued to be given, and also preserved, as the history of the people produced them, and their circumstances required additional revelation.

THE WRITINGS AFTER MOSES

The writings of Moses were deposited in the ark or in some other safe place, and most sacredly guarded. Joshua wrote when it became necessary, and added the important facts of the growing history. His book was added to the five previously written, and thus was formed the Hexateuch. The first six books of the Bible contain the law, the religious ceremonies to be observed, and the noteworthy history of the nation: and for centuries afterwards these formed the inspired book for these Israelites in their new and conquered land.

The Books of the Judges, Ruth, and Samuel, are also almost entirely historical, and cover a period of time generally estimated at about four hundred years after the entrance to Canaan. The altered conditions of the people are clearly set forth in the recorded history contained in these books. The government of the kingdom by judges, the increased liberties enjoyed by both rulers and people, their contamination by the idolatrous worship of their heathen neighbors, and their ultimate desire for a monarch to rule over them, are all fully described. That they were afterwards preserved to the nation is evident from the references made, by the successive writers of the Scriptures, to Moses and Aaron, to the commandments, and the ordinances which had been left for the people, as also from the development of the religious life and history of the Israelites therein revealed.

GREATEST PERIOD OF JUDAIC HISTORY

As we read the Books of the Kings, we find higher ideals concerning both self-government and God had been reached. This record to posterity is also an epitomized history covering another period of 450 years from the last days of King David to the beginning of the exile of the Israelites into Babylon. A single paragraph in the closing verses of this book records an incident which throws much light on the time when it was written. In 2 Kings 25:27, we read, ". . . Evil-merodach king of Babylon in the year that he began to reign did lift up the head of Jehoiachin king of Judah out of prison." ". . . and he did eat bread continually before him all the days of his life" (verse 29). Now there is abundance of history to show that this reign began 561 years before Christ. Therefore, if we suppose the reign reached the limit of an ordinary generation, the latter part at least of the book must have been written between 561 and 538 B.C. And this period of time of which the Book or Books of Kings contain the history, is most interesting in value to all lovers of the Bible, and should be so also to all who appreciate literature. During those centuries, some of the greater prophets spoke their matchless utterances, the Psalms, inimitable as poetic gems, were written and sung, the magnificent Temple of Solomon was built, and its gorgeous services, typical and predictive of the coming Messiah and our glorious Christianity, were inaugurated. These 500 years—from the eleventh century B.C. to the Captivity—form the richest period in Jewish literature, the most spiritual era of the Jewish church, and as a consequence the grandest epoch of the nation's checkered history.

The Proverbs and Ecclesiastes were also written during this period. The Books of Daniel, Ezekiel, Jeremiah, and Esther were written during the Captivity. Ezra, Nehemiah, and probably Chronicles were written after the return from Babylon to Judea, or between the fifth and fourth centuries B.C., though the Chronicles contain the genealogy of the Hebrew race, as also the brief history of that nation.

After the return of the Israelites from captivity, there is an unbroken connection between the Bible and contemporary literature. There was ready access to the Old Testament Scriptures in the service of the second Temple. Nehemiah and Ezra, who represented and conserved in their age all that was best in Jewish life, were contemporaries of Herodotus. Therefore, the writings of the various authors of the Old Testament Scriptures are placed within the reach of all, and as matters of history, are at least as reliable as that seldom disputed Egyptian historian. King Josiah discovered the Scripture writings before the Captivity; Ezra afterwards read the law, and with Nehemiah, and the great men of the Jewish synagogue formed a canon of Old Testament Scriptures about 420 years before Christ. These were afterwards read daily in the synagogue and Temple service.

BIBLE BOOKS NOT CHRONOLOGICAL

However, the books of the Old Testament were not written in the order of time which their arrangement in the Bible seems to indicate. It seems beyond question that the books of the later prophets were written *before* the Books of Kings. Isaiah had doubtless written about three centuries before the Jewish canon of Scripture was formed. Joel, Hosea, and Amos were his contemporaries. Nahum, Habakkuk, and Zephaniah had been dead for over 150 years. But probably without any regard to the order in which they were written, Nehemiah and others collected and arranged them, and placed them in the library of the Temple in which form they have been transmitted to posterity.

However, the Book of Job requires a special word in passing. It contains scarcely one word which justifies its having been placed where it is among the other books of the Bible. There is nothing Jewish in it. In every particular, in style, form, and matter it differs essentially from all the other books of the Bible. It has no religious types to set forth, no history to narrate, only that of a lone man's blood-red struggles with the woes of life, as he battles to reconcile them philosophically with the hidden benevolence of his God.

The strongest evidence places Job between Abraham and Moses, or about seventeen hundred years before Christ. Job's comforters, Eliphaz, Bildad, and Elihu— were without doubt descendants of Abraham, who occupied the territory towards the Persian Gulf. Indeed, it is of the highest probability that they lived in the days immediately following Abraham, and long before Moses, though the book is placed long after the Pentateuch.

For four centuries before Christ nothing was added to the Hebrew Bible. Through this stormy period which began upon the division of the Empire of Alexander the Great, when Palestine became a province of Syria, down to our Saviour's coming, these books were most providentially preserved. Though many attempts were made to destroy every sacred roll of the Jewish people, the Septuagint version of the Old Testament Scriptures was given, a translation which secured certainty to their existence until the birth of our Lord.

WHEN WAS THE NEW TESTAMENT WRITTEN?

The New Testament Scriptures are commonly believed to have been written in the order in which we have them in the Bible. But that is a popular misunder-

standing of the facts. Several epistles were written before any of the Gospels, and the Gospel by John is the
latest production of the sacred books.

The earliest of the New Testament writings is the first
letter by Paul to the Thessalonians, which was written
about the year 51 of the Christian era, and his second
epistle to the same church followed soon after. In the
spring of the year A.D. 52, he wrote his First and Second
letters to the Corinthians, and in 58 he wrote his Epistle
to the Galatians. The following year he wrote his cele-
brated letter to the Romans. During his imprisonment he
wrote to the Colossians, the Ephesians, the Philippians,
and to Philemon. After his release from his first imprisonment, he seems to have gone westward as far as Spain,
and then east as far as Asia Minor, preaching the Gospel;
during this time he wrote his first letters to Timothy and
Titus. Soon afterwards he was rearrested, and again
thrown into a Roman dungeon, where, in the spring of
A.D. 68, a short time before his death, he wrote the Second Epistle to Timothy.

The Gospel by Mark must have been written before
the year 70, and those of Matthew and Luke before the
year 80. The Acts of the Apostles were written before the
Gospel by Luke, and the Epistles of John—also the
Revelation—were written before John's Gospel. Probably all the books of the Bible were concluded by A.D. 80.

HOW WAS THE BIBLE WRITTEN?

And how were the Scriptures written? The answer to
this question is just as important as the other already so
briefly considered. It must be apparent to all that the
human writers must be acknowledged as factors in the
production of the Bible. Various were the ways in which

they were used by the divine Spirit in preparing His revelation. Oral tradition, compilation from historic records were used as well as revelation. The use of such means does not in any sense impair the inspiration of Scripture. "All scripture is given by inspiration . . ." (2 Timothy 3:16), i.e., given as true—though it may be from uninspired sources. "Given by inspiration" surely cannot mean that God is the source and author of *all* contained in the Bible. Such an interpretation of inspiration would seem to make God responsible for the lies Satan told Job, and for a great many other ungodly sayings contained in the book.

It is as injurious as it is needless to confound inspiration and revelation. Inspiration may only suggest, recall, and guide in securing and imparting knowledge already possessed. But it must mean that the writer was supernaturally assisted in making the record accurate. Revelation, however, is the divine Spirit uncovering the unknown to the writer so that it is seen. The traditions of men, the records of history, and revelations from God—all given by inspiration—were the ways in which the world received our Bible.

The compilers of these records, or scribes—as they were called—kept and multiplied them with the greatest care and toil. Writing upon stones, skins, or parchment, and by the pen are the two forms of chirography known to have been in use, for some centuries before the earliest books of the Bible were written. The Ten Commandments were written on stone, and, with the other sacred writings, were copied upon fine skins of leather sewed together in strips, or upon a substance resembling modern paper manufactured from the reeds which grew on the banks of the river Nile. These strips of vellum or papyrus were about four inches in width, and only a few inches in length; they were joined together laterally, and made as long as the writing might require. Thus the roll of which we read so much was formed. The text upon the roll was usually written in columns corresponding to the original pieces of the vellum. Each piece was read in its order, and rolled, when read, upon a stick held in the left hand, while the new columns would appear in the right. This is the form of the sacred books as possessed by the Jews and early Christians, from which were read the Law and the prophets, the Gospels, and all the New Testament writings.

THE LANGUAGES OF THE BIBLE

The original characters in which the Old Testament was written were the old Hebrew excepting the Books of Daniel, Ezekiel, Esther, and Ezra which were partly written in Chaldaic and Aramaic. The writing was a continuous formation of letters without vowels, or periods, to indicate either the sounds of the words, or the sense of the passage. While the Hebrew was a living language, this occasioned little inconvenience, but in view of these linguistic peculiarities, it is a wonder the verbal errors of copyists (which assuredly exist in the present manuscripts) are so few and unimportant. And, under divine guidance, much is due to the efforts of Ezra, Nehemiah, and Massorah for the vocalization, pronunciation, division, and purity of the text, and the development of the language as we now possess it in the Old Testament Scriptures.

The New Testament text was given in similar forms, but by the time it was written the facilities for writing and copying had greatly improved upon those in the days of the Old Testament writers. The New Testament was written originally in Greek without punctuation, or arrangement of the chapters or verses, and the earliest manuscripts reveal two kinds of writing called *uncial* and *cursive*. The uncial is of a large round letter resembling modern capitals, while the cursive is smaller and resembles our present day writing called *round hand*. So numerous were the copyists that before the close of the first century there was at least one copy of the Gospels, and of the epistles, with letters from other early Christian fathers, possessed by all the Christian churches. From these original sources, and by these ways, and in those times, did mankind receive this priceless heritage from heaven. By the diligent hands of the transcriber, through the untiring devotion of those faithful servants of God, and the unerring guidance of the Omniscient Spirit we, at the cost of untold treasures and blood, have thus received this unspeakable gift of the eternal God.

By Whom Was the Bible Written?

For the prophecy came not . . . by the will of man:
but holy men of God spake as they were moved by the
Holy Ghost.

2 Peter 1:21

Someone once said, "A good man could not have written the Bible if he would, and a bad man would not have
written it if he could." We believe the logical answer to
the above question is contained in this epigrammatic
statement. For good men to have written it, and accre-
dited their writings to others than those who wrote, actually would have been to practice deception which, in
such a momentous matter, good men would find impossible to do. For, though we allow that a low moral tone,
and confused conceptions of a lofty motive governed
those writers, they were at least sufficiently human to
understand that one of the certainties of life is the discovery of hypocrisy. The sixty-six books of the Bible
were written by about thirty different writers whose
identity may be known by the ordinary rules which govern the discovery of authors with whom the age is not
personally acquainted.

I have a young friend who, as an engineer, sails the
southern seas. When he writes to me, I know from where
and from whom the letter comes by the government
stamp upon it, by the style of his writing, and the contents of his letters. And these writers of Scripture have
been identified and made known to reasonable religious

people with a satisfactory measure of exactness by similar marks. These marks or evidence have often been ridiculed as inadequate to show the authorship of the Bible. But I have no desire to introduce here any that would not be accepted as valid in the highest courts of the land.

Jurists tell us that "documents found in a place in which, and under the care of persons with whom, such papers might naturally and reasonably be expected to be found, or in the possession of persons having an interest in them, are precisely the custody which gives authenticity to documents found within it."

This statement is founded on the undying principles of equity and justice, and is the basic principle of law practice throughout the civilized world. This evidence is as admissible in proving the authorship as the truthfulness of the Scriptures. It will be possible for us to look into only a few of the most important books of the Bible and endeavor to discover who wrote them by adducing legitimate evidence on their behalf. Those less disputed ones which may not be considered, we shall take for granted according to the rule by which the greater proves the less.

BOOK OF JOB

The authors were all human, and each in writing retained his individuality, though all their writings were given under inspiration of God. Let us begin with the oldest book, the Book of Job. That Job wrote this book seems apparent from the fact that only such a man *could* write it. Keeping in mind the universally acknowledged fact that each inspired writer exercised fully his faculties in declaring his message, the reader should be easily convinced that only a Job who lived in the age of Job, who knew what Job knew, and suffered as he suffered, could have written that matchless poem of human experience and Divine Providence.

There are many good reasons why neither Moses nor Solomon could have written it. They lived in another place and period of the world's history than the author. The writer of it lived in the times of the eastern patriarchs, and in the days of the so-called giants, and of the philosophic discussions of the sons of the east. The mode of life and thought revealed in the book is distinctively Arabian, just as the style of speech and thought in the *Canterbury Tales* is Chaucerian. In Job there are mentioned the worship of the sun, moon, and stars; but there is no word about the worship of idols. Riches are set forth or estimated in value by cattle. The kind of coin prevalent in that age is distinctly named. No sacrifices such as are named in the Pentateuch are spoken about. No reference whatever is made to the Mosaic law, and none to the Exodus. It contains not a solitary allusion to a Jew, or a Hebrew; to the Holy Land, to Jerusalem, to the Tabernacle, or to the Temple—all of which would indicate that the book was written previous to the age of Moses.

It is also of the highest probability that some of those named in the book lived in the days immediately following Abraham. In Genesis 36:4–10, mention is made of Eliphaz as a son of Esau, and it is well known that Esau and his descendants lived in Mount Seir in the east. Another comforter is named Bildad, the Shuhite, which appellation doubtless connects him with Shuah, one of the sons of Abraham by Keturah, and all these sons occupied the country towards the Persian Gulf. Elihu, the

Buzite, was also another comforter, and was probably a descendant of Nahor, who was the founder of the Buzites, and a relative of Abraham. The land owned by Buz is spoken of as "the land of Uz," which was the land where Job dwelt. In *Smith's Bible Dictionary* we are informed that Job had previously borne the name of Jobab, but like the names of Abraham, Jacob, and Joshua, it was changed, and that he was identical with Jobab, the prince of Edom. Therefore the preponderance of evidence shows that the book belongs to the times of Eliphaz, Bildad, and Elihu, who were descendants of Abraham, and contemporaries of Job; and that Job was its author.

MOSES, AUTHOR OF THE PENTATEUCH

The next to be considered is the authorship of the first five books of the Bible called the Pentateuch. Generally speaking, the authorship of these books is ascribed to Moses, excepting, of course, the account of his own death, and a few minor matters attributed to Joshua. The popular reason given is "they were called the books of Moses"; but that is not by any means the principal or only one.

There was no one either before or after the exile of Israel so well qualified as Moses to write them. It has never been disputed that "he was learned in all the learning of the Egyptians," and some of these books give evidence of such learning, which is now known to have been considerable. As the deliverer of the Israelite people, he was acquainted with their needs, their rights, and their history. He lived in a great crisis of the history of his own people; he had been the prime mover in many of their noble deeds, and he, as their leader, would at

least be acquainted with whatever historic documents
existed. Thus he was exceptionally well qualified by his
position to describe accurately the Arab life of his own
ancestors, the exact condition of Egyptian civilization,
the deliverance of Israel from bondage, the subsequent
trials and teachings in their wilderness life. He was their
hero; he had led them to freedom, and was pointing
them to Canaan to win their promised rights by the
sword. He had to justify their mission as a people fulfilling a high destiny, and through whom he proclaimed to
the proud nations, "all the families of the earth should be
blessed."

Never did man hear a louder call; seldom has a man
had such qualifications to write the history of the origin
and development of a nation. It is strange to read denials
of the Mosaic authorship of these books made for the
alleged purpose of removing the miraculous from the
Bible, and in consequence making it more acceptable to
unbelievers. For, it is beyond question, that by placing
the authorship of the first five books of the Bible after the
Exile, the miraculous element in their production is
greatly increased. For instance, if Moses made a record
of many of these events recorded in the Pentateuch as
they occurred, and the accuracy of the record was assured by divine superintendence, there is less of the
miraculous required for him to make the record than
there would be to reveal the facts to another writer one
thousand years after the events, the time when the objectors to the Mosaic authorship claim they were written.

History shows that the Israelites one thousand years
after Moses were entirely separated from Egypt. Their
associations were then Babylonian, Syrian, and Persian.
It would, therefore, be as reasonable to expect Tolstoi,

the Russian, to write without documents or tradition or divine revelation an accurate history of Tammany Hall, or of the American Constitution, as it would be for a writer in that age to write these books. It is readily granted they contain some Babylonian and Assyrian elements, the causes of which shall be stated in future chapters. But on the whole—as already mentioned—the books of Moses are Egyptian books colored with the desert life of the Israelites, revealing the needs and claims; and the relation of these people to one another, and to God; and their great destiny among the nations of the earth, and only a Moses could have written them. Indeed, the theories of our hypercritical friends seem infinitely more bottomless than those of the most orthodox.

The internal evidence of the books when further examined supports even more strongly the Mosaic authorship. Exodus 17:14 says, "The Lord said unto Moses, Write this for a memorial in a book, and rehearse it in the ears of Joshua . . . ." In the same book, in chapter 34:27, 28, we read, "And the Lord said unto Moses, Write thou these words: for after the tenor of these words I have made a covenant with thee and with Israel." In Numbers 33:2 he said, "And Moses wrote their goings out, according to their journeyings by the commandment of the LORD." In Deuteronomy 31:9, 22 we read, "Moses wrote this law . . . . Moses, therefore, wrote this song the same day . . . ." (*See also* verse 24.) And in addition to this evidence we have nearly every writer in the Bible testifying that Moses wrote these books, and the words of the spotless Jesus verify them all. Surely the testimony of Christ ought to be sufficient proof of their Mosaic authorship to any but a thoroughgoing rationalist, for His spotless character is the seal of His truth.

AUTHORSHIP OF OTHER OLD TESTAMENT BOOKS

We come now to the consideration of the authors of the Books of Joshua, Judges, Ruth, and Samuel. That Joshua wrote the book bearing his name has seldom been seriously disputed. It has generally been classified with the five books ascribed to Moses as a part of the early history of the Israelites in Canaan, and its authorship stands or falls with them. For, if the Pentateuch was not written till after the exile, it is impossible to believe that the Book of Joshua with its subsequent history could have been written before it. However, it may be premature to enter upon an elaborate defense of Joshua until Moses has been disposed of. And judging from the recent utterances of one of the opponents to the Mosaic authorship, Joshua is likely to prove as formidable a support to that authorship as he was to the Mosaic wars.

The Book of Judges takes up the history of the Israelite people from the death of Joshua to the death of Samuel and was written by the latter. The contents of the first part of the book are almost indisputable proof of this. That it contains the statement "In those days there was no king in Israel . . ." (Judges 17:6) is no proof that the writer lived at a later date than Samuel. It may only serve to show the fact that no king had as yet been given to Israel.

The Book of Ruth which has been fitly termed a "beautiful epic poem of domestic life," was formerly an appendix of the Book of Judges, and was composed by the same author. This is borne witness to by Josephus,

Origen, and Jerome; and the weight of evidence today is overwhelmingly in favor of Samuel. The Book or Books of Samuel are called so, more because the writer treats of him and his times, than because he wrote them. Their authorship is generally believed to be uncertain, and there is abundant evidence in the book itself to show that it was not written until after the kingdom was divided in Rehoboam's time. The most ancient tradition of its authorship is that the first twenty-four chapters were written by Samuel, and, at a later date, perhaps some prophet—Nathan or Gad—edited the remaining portion. Many modern scholars adopt this view, and the Scriptures themselves which, as evidence, ought to be of still greater value, support it in 1 Chronicles 29:29 by saying, "Now the acts of David the king, first and last, behold, they are written in the book of Samuel the seer, and in the book of Nathan the prophet, and in the book of Gad the seer." But of this book as with some others in the Bible, we can only agree with these words: "He that has a piece of gold of right weight, and stamped with the king's image, cares not to know who minted it."

The Kings, Lamentations, and Jeremiah were written by that prophet. The Books of Kings, which like those of Samuel were originally one, and for a time were united with the Books of the Chronicles, are records of the kings of Judah and Israel compiled and completed by the prophet down to the Captivity, or to the last of the Jewish royal rulers. The Lamentations and Jeremiah contain brief accounts of the sufferings of the nation, the warnings of God to it in its decay, and His earnest invitations to repentance. Josephus and the writers of the Talmud support the Jeremianic authorship of the Lamentations, and the modern critical school favor it.

The objections urged against it are, the absence in some portions of the precarious evidence of Jeremiah's words and style, and his so-called unnatural pastime of busying himself with the poetic art in such calamitous days. But the criticisms are not well founded, for the book shows his own style to be very marked in most chapters. If he had a chance to reply to the charge of "unnatural indifference," he might say with Abraham Lincoln when charged with levity during the Civil War that "but for such a source of relief, grief would have killed me." Concerning the Book of Jeremiah we only quote the beautiful and accurate words of Wordsworth that "his prophecies are his autobiography," which fact is an indisputable proof of his authorship.

Most of the Proverbs were written and/or collected by Solomon as was also the Book of Ecclesiastes, or "the Preacher." This was written after his weary soul had struggled through selfishness, sensuality, and perplexity into a calm, pure peace. He probably also wrote the Song of Solomon. This last as shown in the Book of Kings (1 Kings 4:32; Song of Solomon 1:1) is closely related to the Proverbs, which are universally conceded to the wise king, and links inseparably the authorship of both.

The Book of Psalms which contains the sweetest of the Hebrew nation's poetry, the spiritual songs of the Jewish Church, and a reflection of the religious and irreligious experience of the writers, has several authors. Of these psalms, after the most searching criticism, the consensus of opinion shows seventy-nine written by David, one by Moses, one by Solomon, twelve by Asaph, one by Heman, and one by Ethan. The remaining fifty-one are anonymous; eleven of them were written for the sons of Korah; fifteen are called pilgrim songs; eleven, hal-

lelujah psalms beginning with the words "praise the
Lord," and Psalm 136 in which the mercy of the Lord is
sung twenty-six times.

The authors of the minor, or lesser books of the
prophets we must pass by with the statement that excepting Daniel, they are almost universally believed to
have been the writers of the several books whose names
they bear. Their messages and style are variously
adapted to the nature of their various missions, are fully
in harmony with their personality, with the times in
which they lived, and of which they wrote.

DISPUTE OVER ISAIAH AND DANIEL

It is, however, very different with the Books of Isaiah
and Daniel, as the authorship of these has been most
fiercely disputed. The story of Jonah has been laughed at
by scoffing unbelievers, but Christian(?) rationalists
have discredited the authorship of Isaiah and Daniel
largely because they disbelieve their prophecies. For
example, these objectors admit Isaiah wrote twenty-six
chapters of the book bearing his name, but when they
come to the prophecy concerning Cyrus and his kingdom, rather than believe in the prophecy, they say, "He
is not the author of the remaining chapters." "A second
Isaiah," say they, "some unknown writer in the time of
Cyrus wrote these."

If this were true, it is not passing strange that a writer
equal to Isaiah, their prophet, almost the peer of David
in sacred song, a leader of the Jewish people with the
clearest Messianic message on his lips, should have
been "unknown" to Israel? Think of a Churchill being
forgotten one hundred and fifty years hence by the
British; of the name of Lincoln never being found in an

archive of the United States, and then believe this
counselor of Jewish kings, unsurpassed of Jewish
statesmen—this messenger of the Messianic kingdom
upon which "Israel's hope" rested and who wrote this
latter part of the Book of Isaiah—was "unknown"! The
entire book was attributed to Isaiah the son of Amoz, by
the great Synagogue composed of such illustrious men as
Ezra, Nehemiah, Zechariah, and Haggai. For centuries
after the Captivity, the book was used every Sabbath day
as "the Book of Isaiah," and thirteen out of its sixteen
prophetic readings were selected from the part of the
book objected to by those critics. The author of the first
part of it wrote in the reign of Hezekiah, and the author
of the second part also speaks of the wife of Hezekiah as
a type of the church of God restored.

John the Baptist was the strongest link in the chain
which bound the Jewish church to the New Testament
age prior to the birth of Christ. In telling us through
whom he received his commission as herald of the
matchless Monarch Christ, he quotes from chapter 40 of
Isaiah, "I am the voice of one crying in the wilderness,
Make straight the way of the Lord, as said [Isaiah the
prophet]" (John 1:23). Our Lord when on earth received
into His holy hands that same roll from which John the
Baptist unwittingly testified to the single Isaiah authorship, and He also read the words as those of Isaiah. As
the writers of the most recent life of Lincoln have shown
that by his style, manner, and matter those letters are
Lincoln's, and not Seward's or Blaine's, so Professor
Franz Delitzsch, one of the foremost of Hebrew scholars
and students of eastern literature, shows that the senten-
tious style and sharp movement of thought, everywhere
discernible in the beginning of Isaiah's book, are but the

prelude to the majestic harmonies in the latter half of it. So that if he wrote the first part—which has not been disputed—it is evident he wrote the whole.

Our Lord and some of His apostles have repeatedly borne witness to Daniel as the author of the book which bears his name, and all Jewish tradition ascribes it to that heroic prophet. The strongest objection to this view is founded upon the fact that the book is written in both the Hebrew and Chaldaic languages. From this, the objectors conclude that there were at least two authors of it. However, if it be remembered that Daniel was a Hebrew who knew both languages; that it would be natural for him to relate the early history of himself and his companions in Hebrew, and write the visions pertaining to the Babylonian empire in the prevailing language of that nation, the objection fades like a star before the sunlight. Moreover, the dual character of the language used, proves it must have been written by a Jew in the Babylonian Captivity. The exact acquaintance of the historic relations, the court manners, and national customs of Daniel's time revealed in the book testify that the author was also a person in high position and distinction in Babylon. It has been also objected that there are historic inaccuracies in the book—though, so far, the statement is supported by more assumption than fact—which could not have been made by a resident author. But a cuneiform tablet discovered in Nineveh shows Belshazzar to have been both a prince and a man of action throughout the nation, and that Daniel was at least so far correct in his history.

With the remark that Ezra and Nehemiah wrote the histories ascribed to them after the return of the Israelites from the Captivity in Babylon, we shall briefly notice the writers of the New Testament Scriptures.

NEW TESTAMENT AUTHORS

Only the authorship of the Epistle to the Hebrews, and the second one ascribed to Peter and the Gospel by John, have been earnestly disputed. It is uncertain who wrote the Epistle to the Hebrews, but the weight of evidence supports the general belief that Peter wrote the second epistle ascribed to him. The accepted authorship of John's Gospel has been fiercely assailed; but we must either accept of John as its author, or that the Gospel is an intentional fraud. The author repeatedly declares himself to have been an eye-witness of the life of Christ (John 1:14; 19:35; 1 John 1:1). It was generally received as John's Gospel fifty years after his death. Marcion, Valentinus, Basilides and other critical writers of the first and second centuries acknowledge its genuineness. Such evidence cannot be explained, if John was not its author.

Of course, the trustworthiness or authenticity of others has been questioned, but not their authorship. Paul wrote thirteen of the twenty-seven New Testament books. Luke wrote The Acts of the Apostles and the Gospel bearing his name, and the others were either written or dictated by those to whom they are ascribed. It has often been asserted there were no Christian writings in the first century, and that it was one of dark superstition of which there is nothing certain or reliable. But the histories of the first four centuries of the Christian era reveal the opposite. Indeed, the pagan and patristic literature, the writings of both apologists and unbelievers of that time illustrate most fully the amazing audacity and groundless assumptions of modern infidelity on this important question.

These New Testament authors were our Lord's biographers and first writers to His infant church. They were as well known to the churches as W. E. Vine is in the Christian world today, and a copy of their writings was in nearly every Christian congregation. The indisputable evidence of this is in the following historic and well known facts. Polycarp was a pupil of Saint John; and Justin Martyr, a disciple of Polycarp, was born ten years before John died. Clement and Barnabas of the beginning of the second century mention in their letters the Epistles of Paul. Tertullian, also of the second century, occupies in his works thirty folio pages by quotations from the autograph writings of these apostles and evangelists.

In the third century Origen, Victorinus, and Dionysius wrote expositions of these writings, and quoted long extracts from the apostles. In the fourth century there existed eleven distinct catalogs of these books with the names of the writers appended. In several church councils of which the last was held at Carthage in 397, there was set forth a list containing all the New Testament books with their authors. These are only a few of many writings which show the first four Christian centuries teemed with testimony most credible to the writers of the New Testament.

ANTI-CHRISTIAN WRITERS

Moreover, as another has remarked, "These books could not have been written in the same language in which we have them if they had not been written before the end of the first century," and therefore by our authors. When Jerusalem was destroyed in A.D. 70, the Jews were rooted out of the land almost stock and branch. Foreigners came to it from all directions, and the former language of the people became a dead language. It became a conglomerate, and in the first quarter of the second century there were few, if any, who could either speak or write the language of the apostles. Indeed any attempt to do so would have failed as entirely as that of Josh Billings to reform the English language by phonetic spelling. Infidel writers of the first four centuries also wrote favoring our authors. The Emperor Julian, known as "the apostate," wrote in 361 a work against Christianity; but he nowhere expressed a doubt as to either the books of Christians or their authors. It is almost certain that had occasion admitted of it, he would have challenged the genuineness of the books.

Porphyry, universally conceded to have been the most formidable opponent to Christianity, wrote in 270, and spoke of Matthew as "their evangelist." In 176, Celsus, esteemed by modern infidels as a wonderful philosopher, wrote a book against Christianity entitled *A True Discourse*, of which Origen has preserved fragments. But so unlike was he to his modern infidel brethren that he admitted the existence of the Christian or New Testament writings, and their genuineness.

Is it unfair to ask, "Was it because he knew more than his present-day successors in unbelief, or was he only more honest than they?" Whatever the reason, it must be apparent to every unprejudiced mind that earnest seekers after truth, who ignore such testimony accessible to the average scholar, are inexcusably guilty of trifling with indisputable evidence which would be convincing in any civil court. Such testimony has been provided in abundance alike by the friends and foes of the lowly Nazarene—our Lord in glory—and it proves that these ". . . holy men of God," to whom their writings were assigned, "spake as they were moved by the Holy Ghost" (2 Peter 1:21).

(These excerpts from *How, When and by Whom Was the Bible Written* by James Todd are used by permission of the publisher, Fleming H. Revell Company.)

SELECTED, CLASSIFIED, AND ANNOTATED BIBLIOGRAPHY

Prepared by David K. Huttar, Ph.D.

This bibliography is intended for students with only an elementary knowledge of Hebrew. It focuses on linguistic tools for Old Testament study, but also suggests readings in background and related materials. General reference works such as Bible dictionaries and encyclopedias are not included, even though they contain valuable articles on many relevant topics. Books marked with an asterisk are especially recommended.

I. **Old Testament Texts**
   A. The Old Testament in Hebrew (with portions in Aramaic)
      *1. Kittel, Rudolf, ed. *Biblia Hebraica.* 9th ed. Württembergische Bibelanstalt, 1954.
         The standard Hebrew Old Testament text.
      2. *Interlineary Hebrew English Psalter.* Grand Rapids, Michigan: Zondervan, 1970.
      3. Berry, George R. *Interlinear Hebrew-English Old Testament: Genesis-Exodus.* Reprint of 1896 ed. Grand Rapids, Michigan: Kregel.
      4. Magil, Joseph. *Englishman's Hebrew Old*

Testament. Grand Rapids, Michigan: Zondervan, 1974.

Interlinear of Genesis–II Samuel.

B. The Old Testament in Greek

*1. Rahlfs, Alfred, ed. *Septuaginta.* 5th ed. Württembergische Bibelanstalt, 1952.

2. *Septuagint Version of the Old Testament, with an English Translation.* Bagster.

Convenient but not as critical as Rahlfs.

II. Concordances

A. To Authorized Version (King James)

1. Young, Robert. *Young's Analytical Concordance to the Bible.* rev. ed. Grand Rapids, Michigan: Eerdmans, 1955.

B. To Hebrew Text (in order of difficulty)

*1. *Englishman's Hebrew and Chaldee Concordance of the Old Testament.* Grand Rapids, Michigan: Zondervan.

Words listed under Hebrew/Aramaic forms but quotations of passages in English.

2. Lisowsky, G. *Konkordanz zum hebraischen Alten Testament.* Württembergische Bibelanstalt, 1958.

Quotations in vocalized Hebrew.

3. Mandelkern, Solomon. *Veteris Testamenti Concordantiae Hebraicae et Chalaicae.* Leipzig, 1896.

Hebrew words arranged according to grammatical form; unvocalized; available in modern reprints.

C. To Greek Text (in order of completeness)

1. Morrish, G. *A Handy Concordance of the Septuagint.* London, 1887.

Context not quoted.

2. Hatch, Edwin. *A Concordance of the Septuagint and Other Greek Versions of the Old Testament*. Reprint. 2 vols. New York: International Publications.
   Quotations in Greek.

III. **Grammars of Hebrew and Aramaic**
   A. Elementary Hebrew. Any of the following may be used.
      1. Finley, Harvey and Isbell, Charles D. *Biblical Hebrew*. Kansas City, Missouri: Beacon Hill, 1975.
      2. Harper, William R. *Elements of Hebrew by an Inductive Method*. Reprint. Chicago: University of Chicago Press, 1974.
      *3. Harris, R. Laird. *Introductory Hebrew Grammar*. Grand Rapids, Michigan: Eerdmans, 1950.
      *4. La Sor, W. Sanford. *Handbook to Biblical Hebrew*. Grand Rapids, Michigan: Eerdmans, 1978.
      5. Mansoor, Menahem. *Biblical Hebrew Step by Step*. Grand Rapids, Michigan: Baker, 1978.
      6. Marks, John H. and Rogers, Virgil M. *Beginner's Handbook to Biblical Hebrew*. Nashville: Abingdon, 1958.
      7. Sellers, Ovid R. and Voight, E. E. *Biblical Hebrew for Beginners*. 12th corr. ed. Naperville, Illinois: Allenson, 1963.
      8. Smith, James M., ed. *Introductory Hebrew: Method and Manual*. rev. ed. Harper, William R. Chicago: University of Chicago Press, 1974.
      9. Weingreen, Jacob. *Practical Grammar for*

Classical Hebrew. 2nd ed. New York: Oxford University Press, 1959.

10. Yates, Kyle M. *Essentials of Biblical Hebrew.* rev. ed. J. J. Owens, ed. New York: Harper & Row, 1955.

B. Grammatical Aids

1. Davidson, Benjamin. *Analytical Hebrew and Chaldee Lexicon.* Grand Rapids, Michigan: Zondervan.

2. Halkin, A. S. *Two Hundred and One Hebrew Verbs Fully Conjugated in All the Forms.* Woodbury, New York: Barron, 1970.

3. Peterson, David E. and Barker, Kenneth L. *Hebrew Old Testament Slidaverb Conjugation Chart.* Grand Rapids, Michigan: Zondervan.

C. Intermediate

1. Rosenthal, Franz. *Grammar of Biblical Aramaic.* New York: International Publications, 1968.

*2. Williams, R. J. *Hebrew Syntax: An Outline.* New York: University of Toronto Press, 1967.

D. Advanced

1. Kautsch, E. and Cowley, A. E. *Gesenius' Hebrew Grammar.* 2nd ed. Gesenius, William, ed. New York: Oxford University Press, 1910.

2. Moscati, Sabatino. *An Introduction to the Comparative Grammar of the Semitic Languages: Phonology and Morphology.* New York: International Publications, 1969.

IV. Dictionaries and Word Studies

A. Dictionaries (in order of difficulty)

*1. Fohrer, Georg, et al., eds. *Hebrew and Aramaic Dictionary of the Old Testament.* Translated by W. A. Johnstone. New York: De Gruyter, 1973.

2. Brown, Francis, et al., eds. *A Hebrew and English Lexicon of the Old Testament.* 2nd ed. William Gesenius. Translated by Edward Robinson. New York: Oxford University Press, 1959.

B. Lexical Aids

1. Landes, George M. *Student's Vocabulary of Biblical Hebrew: Listed According to Frequency and Cognate.* New York: Scribner, 1961.

2. Watts, John D. *Lists of Words Occurring Frequently in the Hebrew Bible.* Grand Rapids, Michigan: Eerdmans, 1960.

C. Word Studies. Although some of the following deal primarily with the New Testament, they usually give Old Testament material as well.

1. Botterweck, G. Johannes and Ringgren, Helmer, eds. *Theological Dictionary of New Testament Theology.* 2 vols. Grand Rapids, Michigan: Eerdmans, 1974.

2. Brown, Colin, ed. *The New International Dictionary of New Testament Theology.* Paternoster, 1975.

*3. Girdlestone, Robert B. *Synonyms of the Old Testament.* (Reprint of 1897 ed.) Grand Rapids, Michigan: Eerdmans, 1948.

4. Kittel, Gerhard and Friedrich, Gerhard, eds. *Theological Dictionary of the New Testa-*

ment. 9 vols. Grand Rapids, Michigan: Eerdmans, 1964–1973.

5. Richardson, Alan. *A Theological Word Book of the New Bible.* New York: Macmillan, 1953.

V. Old Testament Introduction
A. General

1. Archer, Gleeson L. *A Survey of Old Testament Introduction.* Chicago: Moody Press, 1973.

*2. Harrison, Roland K. *Introduction to the Old Testament.* Grand Rapids, Michigan: Eerdmans, 1969.

3. Young, Edward J. *An Introduction to the Old Testament.* rev. ed. Grand Rapids, Michigan: Eerdmans, 1958.

B. Text (in order of difficulty)

*1. Ap-Thomas, D. R. *A Primer of Old Testament Text Criticism.* Philadelphia: Fortress, 1966.

2. Wurthwein, E. *The Text of the Old Testament.* Blackwell, 1957.

3. Cross, Frank M. *The Ancient Library of Qumran and Modern Biblical Studies.* New York: Doubleday, 1958.

C. Canon

1. Harris, R. Laird. *Inspiration and Canonicity of the Bible.* Grand Rapids, Michigan: Zondervan, 1971.

VI. Geography

*A. Aharoni, Yohanan and Avi-Yonah, Michael. *The Macmillan Atlas.* New York: Macmillan, 1968.

B. May, Herbert G. and Hunt, G. H. *Oxford Bible Atlas.* 2nd ed. New York: Oxford University Press, 1974.

C. Wright, George E. and Filson, Floyd V., eds. *The Westminster Historical Atlas to the Bible.* rev. ed. Philadelphia: Westminster Press, 1956.

VII. Archaeology and Customs

*A. Devaux, Roland. *Ancient Israel.* 3 vols. New York: McGraw-Hill, 1965.

B. Harrison, R. K. *The Archaeology of the Old Testament.* New York: Harper & Row, 1963.

C. Kitchen, K. A. *Ancient Orient and Old Testament.* Downers Grove, Illinois: Inter-Varsity Press, 1966.

D. Pfeiffer, Charles F., ed. *Biblical World: A Dictionary of Biblical Archaeology.* Grand Rapids, Michigan: Baker Book House, 1964.

E. Pritchard, J. B., ed. *Ancient Near Eastern Texts Relating to the Old Testament With Supplement.* 3rd ed. Princeton, New Jersey: Princeton University Press, 1969.

F. Thomas, D. Winton, ed. *Documents From Old Testament Times.* New York: Harper & Row, 1961.

G. Thompson, John A. *Bible and Archaeology.* Grand Rapids, Michigan: Eerdmans, 1962.

*H. Yamauchi, E. M. *The Stones and the Scriptures.* Washington, D.C.: Holman, 1977.

VIII. Old Testament History

A. Bright, John. *A History of Israel.* 2nd ed. Philadelphia: Westminster Press, 1972.

B. Bruce, Fredrick F., ed. *Israel and the Nations.*

Grand Rapids, Michigan: Eerdmans, 1963.
C. Harrison, Roland K. *Old Testament Times.*
Grand Rapids, Michigan: Eerdmans, 1970.

IX. **Old Testament Theology**
A. Davidson, A. B. *The Theology of the Old Testament.* Philadelphia: R. West, 1952.
B. Eichrodt, W. *Theology of the Old Testament.* 2 vols. Translated by J. Baker. Philadelphia: Westminster Press, 1961.
*C. Payne, J. Barton. *Theology of the Older Testament.* Grand Rapids, Michigan: Zondervan, 1962.
D. Pedersen, Johannes. *Israel: Its Life and Culture.* Reprint. 4 vols. New York: Oxford University Press, 1973.
E. Vriezen, Theodorus C. *An Outline of Old Testament Theology.* New ed. Newton Center, Massachusetts: Branford, 1974.

X. **Commentaries (in order of difficulty)**
*A. Wiseman, D. J., ed. *Tyndale Old Testament Commentaries.* Downers Grove, Illinois: Inter-Varsity Press.
*B. Harrison, R. K., ed. *The New International Commentary on the Old Testament.* Grand Rapids, Michigan: Eerdmans.
C. Keil, O. E. and Delitzsch, F. *Biblical Commentary on the Old Testament.* Reprint. Grand Rapids, Michigan: Eerdmans, 1949.
D. Albright, W. F. and Freedman, D. N., eds. *The Anchor Bible.* New York: Doubleday.
E. Briggs, C. A., Driver, S. R., and Plummer, A., eds. *The International Critical Commentary.* New York: Scribner.